M000168437

Nostradamus'
Dream Book

Nostradamus' Dream Interpretations

All rights (whole or part) reserved, especially concerning translation and dissemination through public lectures, films, radio, television, any type of sound carrier, copying, photographic reproduction or any other form of duplication, or storage by computer.

Copyright © 1998 by Dietlinde Arzt-Wegman

For more information, contact:
Vasitha Publications,
P.O. Box 70013,
2441 Lakeshore Rd. W.,
Oakville, ON L6L 6M9
Canada

fax: (905) 827-8281
http://www.nostradamusdreams.com

Canadian Cataloguing in Publication Data
Arzt-Wegman, D.
Nostradamus' Dream Interpretations

ISBN 0-9686022-0-7

Printed in Canada
by Webcom Ltd.
Toronto

Table of Contents

Note From the Author

The following sections of this book are direct translations of the German Original:
Neuestes vollständiges and grösstes egyptisches Traumbuch, wahrhafte Auslegung aller Träume.
Last published in 1928.

- A-Z Interpretation of Dream Images
- Chart of Lucky and Unlucky Days
- Meaning of Dreams According to the Zodiac
- Birthmonth—Characteristics
- Fingernail—Characteristics

In this revised edition, I have included my own notes:

- Nostradamus
- Foreword
- What are Dreams?
- One Step Further
- To Nostradamus
- Epilogue

It will help the reader to receive the language of Dreams and to further understand the "World of Dreams."

Finally, for those of us striving today to obtain the knowledge and wisdom that Nostradamus exhibited over 400 years ago, I include in the Epilogue information on some further reading that is invaluable in that regard.

Dita

Nostradamus

Nostradamus, the world's most renowned prophet, was born Michel de Notredame in the little town of Saint Remy, Provence, France, on December 14, 1503.

His life ended on July 2, 1556.

Besides being an astrologer and astronomer, he was also a successful medical doctor, and was appointed official physician to King Charles IX of France. He was also the King's personal astrologer. In 1547 he began making predictions, amazing everyone—including the King—with his accuracy.

In 1555, he compiled these visions (many that he foresaw hundreds of years into the future) into a book called *Centuries*. Among his most remarkable predictions were the assassination of John F. Kennedy, the collapse of world communism, space flights, and man's landing on the moon.

More than half of his prophecies relate to events that will happen now, as well as those that will occur far beyond our present era.

Foreword

The extensive Egyptian Dream Book by Nostradamus was last published in Germany in 1928. This treasure has been in my possession for many years; thus I have had many opportunities to challenge the accuracy and truthfulness of the interpretations. Over and over again I have been amazed by Nostradamsus' prophesies and the direction they have given me in foretelling the meaning behind my own dreams. My decision to translate the book, was following my inner voice, so that others can appreciate the experience themselves.

With this revised edition, I call it back to life, translated into English for the first time ever.

Nostradamus' Dream Interpretations will escort you on your journey through life. It can be a tremendous help, warning of difficult times or predicting the joyful ones that are inevitable in everyone's life. To acknowledge it day by day is an experience in itself, because if you are aware of what is imminent, you can prepare yourself to take on the task. Now, using your free will, you have the chance to prevent unpleasant events, or to fully enjoy the privilege of experiencing the good fortune ahead.

With only a few words, Nostradamus addresses the essence of the meaning of a dream. Long explanations are unnecessary, because "conceived" dreams have only a prophetic message. In contrast, the scientific approach often looks at how a dream is "produced" by the intellect to determine the cause of a person's mental state. Many pages of writing are required to analyse the person's state of mind. Since produced dreams do not foretell what lies ahead, this type of interpretation is a totally different subject.

Nostradamus achieved a full understanding of the laws of creation and how they are connected to our daily lives. This knowledge, combined with his mastery of both astrology and astronomy, gave him the wisdom to write his DREAM BOOK, a gift to the world.

What are Dreams?

Dreams escort us on our trip through life, from birth until the end of our time on earth. They originate from the depths of our soul and reveal themselves to us pictorially, without words. We spend almost a third of our lives sleeping, entering the subconscious mind, and yet we pay hardly any attention to that aspect of our life. In fact, these days that part of our existence is almost totally ignored.

Those who delve intensively into the Dream Phenomenon are astounded by the riches discovered within their soul, and thus come to understand the meaning and importance of dreams in our lives.

There are two types of dreams. The first is "produced" by the conscious brain. These are the dreams that psychiatrists and psychotherapists often use to analyse a person's state of mind. These produced dreams have no prophetic meaning.

The second type of dream is "conceived" by the subconscious mind, which is connected to the intuition. It is these conceived dreams that Nostradamus referred to in his predictions.

In order to understand the meaning of these conceived dreams we must have the right tool, or key, to open the door. We can then cross the threshold into that mystic, unknown world of the beyond. For thousands of years, dreams and their meanings have been among the greatest mysteries of human existence. One of the oldest civilizations to explore the meaning of dreams was Egypt. Documents showing this, dating back almost 4000 years, are kept in the British Museum in London. Egyptians and Assyrers were masters in dream interpretation, and on that knowledge the Greeks and Romans continued to build.

Nostradamus—astrologer, astronomer, and the greatest gifted SEER of all times—mastered and understood the universal laws in creation. That knowledge enabled him to open the door to the subconscious with his own key, and to give us, through his wisdom, the true interpretation of dreams.

One Step Further
Receiving The Language of Dreams

To receive the language of dreams you need to learn how to separate the two active brains. There is no definite pattern or method to follow, but here is a technique to try.

When you fall asleep, you put your conscious brain to rest; or, you may say it is "set on low-energy." Learn to leave it as such. Don't dwell on the happenings or events of the day. Give your brain the well-deserved rest it needs. Relax. Let the subconscious mind, the intuition, go to work.

Begin by focusing on some joyful events from your past. For instance, you may want to think back and collect memories from your childhood: the innocent, carefree times and the warmth and protected love you received from your mother. In that humble mood, at peace with yourself, be grateful. Let your spirit or soul speak and send your thoughts in gratitude up to your creator. That peace of mind will enable you to open the channels so that perceiving can flow easily to the intuitive brain and be recognized. In this state of mind you will be able to connect with a different level of existence—namely, the spiritual world. Now, since you know that you are relying on other influences, besides the productivity of your intellect, you are resting peacefully, with a cleared mind.

In this relaxed and humble state you will travel through the different levels of the sleep process until you fall into "deep sleep" where dreams are being formed. (We could call this the waiting station, where we retrieve our dreams.) I have used the word "fall" deliberately, because I am sure that almost everyone in their life, while drifting off to sleep, has had the feeling of falling. Your body responds with a convulsion. This is the moment that your soul takes off to the realm in which prophetic dreams can be reached.

As you become mindful of using or activating the small brain (the intuitive) more often, you will find it very easy to distinguish and recognize which dreams you should pay attention to. In these dreams you will see distinct pictures, without spoken words, of what lies ahead.

I suggest that, in the beginning (until you have trained your mind) you keep a notebook and pen on your night table. As soon as you begin to awaken from your sleep, concentrate on—and hold onto—the pictures you were seeing so vividly just seconds before. Then, using the paper and pen, quickly write down descriptions of the images that caught your attention the most.

It is important that you train yourself to concentrate on the visual images from your dreams before you even begin to realize it is time to get up—before you begin smelling the coffee and thinking of your busy schedule, thus interrupting the transmission process from the subconscious to the active brain. Once your mind becomes active, it is very difficult to recall the pictures your dreams provided because your conscious brain takes over. Forcing yourself to remember will be almost impossible because the images could have been erased.

Before I close this chapter, I would like to share with you a phrase written by the well-known German philosopher, C.G. Lichtenberg:

"It belongs to the privilege of every human being
knowing that we dream, and having the KNOWLEDGE of it.
The dream is part of our life, and should be connected
with our daily life to become ONE.
Only that should we call 'THE REAL LIFE'.**"**

Interpretation of
Picture Images in Dreams

A

Abbess, to see a female abbot:
Haughtiness and arrogance are detrimental to your character.

Abbott, to see one in his robes:
Annoyance.

Abundance, to experience:
You are holding onto false hopes.

Abduction, being or witnessing:
An unexpected, imminent marriage.

Accident:
Relief from worries.

Accusation, being accused by others:
Restlessness and discontent.

Accusing others:
Troubled success.

Acorns, gathering:
Profit.

Acorn, receiving a wreath of acorn leaves:
Distinction and honour.

Acquainted, getting to know someone:
There will be loss or affliction.

Adder, seeing this kind of snake:
An unpleasant and dangerous acquaintance.

Adultery:
Horrendous disagreements

Adultery, withstanding the temptation of:
Triumph over your enemies.

Advertisement, seeing or reading:
Disgrace.

Advertisement or public notification:
>Work without success or profit.

Advice, giving advice to others:
>Luck in completing difficult business matters.

Advice, receiving:
>You will be deceived.

Air balloon, to see one flying:
>A separation ahead.

Alcoholic, being one:
>Happiness and health.

Almonds, eating them:
>Your nosiness will embarrass you.

Aloe, seeing this plant:
>You will renew an old friendship.

Altar, to see one:
>Comfort and enjoyment.

Amber, seeing this stone as a necklace:
>Gift.

Ambush, falling into an ambush or trap:
>Hardship in business.

Amusement park:
>You will be well and enjoy advantages.

Anchor, to see one:
>Confirmation of hopes.

Anchor, to throw one:
>Great danger.

Anchovy, eating or seeing:
>Good consistent luck.

Angel, to be one:
>Good luck, confirmation of hopes and wishes, welcome news.

Angel, to become one:
>For a healthy person, honour; an ill person, death.

Angry, to become:
>Irreconcilable enemies.

Animals, belonging to you or feeding them:
Happiness and wealth.

Animals, seeing various breeds:
Associations with unknown people.

Animals being tamed:
Patiently overcoming obstacles.

Animals jumping:
Loss of freedom or independence.

Antler, to see these:
Faithlessness and treason.

Ants, to see them:
Much work; achievements recognized and honoured.

Ant hill, stepping on one:
You will find yourself in bad company.

Anvil, seeing one:
A steady job and secure income.

Apostle, to see or speak to one:
Good news.

Apple, to see or eat an exquisite one:
Joy, amusement, long life, good fortune in love, steadfastness and good luck in business matters.

Apple, cutting a tasty apple;
Separation from your boyfriend or girlfriend.

Apple, eating a sour one:
Disputes, arguments, sadness, or false friends.

Apple, seeing many on a tree:
You will have many relatives.

Apple juice, or drinking apple wine:
Vain efforts, arguments, indecency.

Apricots seeing or eating:
A late marriage.

April Fool's Day:
You will experience honour in the near future.

Apron, putting on a beautiful one:
You will receive presents.

Apron, made of silk:
> Fortunate money circumstances.

Arbour, being in one:
> A pleasant acquaintance.

Archery, to span and shoot:
> Comfort in your sorrow.

Archbishop, to see one:
> Rapid death.

Architect, to see one giving instructions:
> A well-managed life

Argument, occurring between friends:
> Declining prosperity.

Argument, winning in one:
> With great effort, your status will improve.

Ark, seeing one:
> You will become annoyed.

Arm, being broken:
> Disaster or death.

Arm, being hairy:
> A huge fortune.

Arm, being wounded:
> Sadness.

Arm, having a huge one:
> Hard work ahead.

Arm, having a small one:
> Falling into poverty.

Arm bandage, to put one or several on:
> You will be sick in bed.

Armchair:
> A comfortable and amusing life.

Armour, to wear:
> Stay away from your enemies.

Arms, seeing many of them:
> Conditions will worsen; great unhappiness.

Arms and weapons, being broken:
   A dispute.

Arms and weapons, to see or own them:
   Happiness and honour.

Arms or weapons, being made:
   Bad times are ahead.

Army, to see one in combat:
   Misery and grief.

Army, to see one marching:
   Mischief and harm approaching.

Arrested, being arrested yourself:
   Obstacles in ventures, fraud and slander.

Arrow, to see one:
   Forthcoming hardship, disagreements.

Arrow, shooting:
   You will steer yourself into bad luck.

Arsenal, to see one:
   War times approaching, unrest.

Artichoke, seeing or eating:
   Quiet suffering, imminent separation.

Ashes, to see:
   A bitter delusion or insult.

Asparagus field:
   Huge gain or profit.

Assets:
   Forthcoming losses.

Audience, having one with a dignitary:
   Happiness and gain.

Authority, seeing a person of authority:
   Bad luck and a lengthy lawsuit.

Avalanche, to witness one:
   Affliction and grief.

Awaken, to see yourself awaken exceptionally early:
   Happiness and forthcoming wealth.

Axe, to see one:
A rebellion, revolt, or bad luck in general.

Axe, to split wood with one:
A split or separation.

B

Bacon (ham, smoked meat), eating or seeing:
death of a friend or relative, pursuit by enemies.

Badger, catching:
loosing your living quarters.

Bagpipe playing, hearing:
joyfulness.

Bag (paper), seeing many:
unfaithfulness.

Bailiff, seeing or talking to:
warning about bad people, difficult keeping the first lover, being tricked in business matters.

Bay-leaf tree:
success in your endeavor.

Bay-leaf picking:
hopes fading away.

Bay-leaf wreath:
coming to honour.

Baked-goods, eating:
means, good times ahead.

Baker or bakery, seeing:
a blessed year.

Baking bread:
good nutritious food.

Baking cookies:
to become useful.

Bake (kneading) trough, empty:
misery

Bake (kneading) trough, full:
wealth.

Baker's oven:
good fortune.

Bald, being:
old age.

Bald-headed person:
derision, scorn.

Ball playing:
good prospect.

Ball-game:
continuous disagreements.

Ball (dance), attending:
special distinction, honour.

Ballet seeing:
deception, cheat.

Balloon seeing:
misfortune lies ahead.

Balcony, standing on:
reciprocate love.

Balsam:
earning praise.

Bandit, seeing:
persecution.

Band-noise, explosion:
ill-fated message.

Banishing someone:
bad luck.

Bank-building:
a flourishing business, security in ventures.

Banker, seeing:
involvement in gossip.

Barefooted running:
body weakness.

Barley, eating:
> health.

Barley, seeing:
> food shortage, worries.

Barn, full:
> sudden, unexpected wealth.

Barracks, seeing:
> secure in traffic.

Barrel, seeing:
> beware of gluttony.

Barrier-gate, breaking:
> returning from abroad.

Basin, in brass or copper:
> faithfulness, loyalty.

Basin, washing yourself:
> cleanliness is the essence of health.

Basket, empty:
> losses.

Basket, closed:
> secrets.

Basket (with handle) carrying:
> worries about the future.

Basket with flowers:
> lucky in love.

Bat, catching:
> ill persons, quick recovery.

Bat, seeing:
> doubtful business success, inconsistent people around you.

Bathtub water, muddy:
> danger of fire.

Bathing, in clear water:
> happiness, health, luck and success in love.

Bathing, in muddy water:
> sorrow, ill-health, bad luck and disappointment.

Bathing, in warm water:
    ill-person, health; healthy person, obstacles in business.

Bathing, in general:
    anger.

Bathing, in the room:
    grief, sorrow.

Battle (fight), attending or seeing:
    having unknown enemies, betrayal in love, being cheated.

Beans, eating or seeing:
    indicating dispute ahead, experiencing misfortune and
    defamation of character.

Beans seeing in full bloom:
    a wish coming true.

Beans, growing:
    a purpose is acknowledged.

Beans, being burned:
    lots of annoyance.

Beans, peeling:
    worries about the future.

Beans, planting:
    new takeover of business.

Bears, seeing:
    suffer from injustice, bad gossip (in general, image is not
    good; furthermore, dreams with hyenas, tigers and wild
    beasts mean misfortune, quarrels, discord).

Beard, black, good looking:
    health.

Beard, grey:
    ill-humour, melancholy.

Beard, long one:
    profit, luck.

Beard, red:
    false friends.

Beard, seeing on a woman:
    annoyance, unpleasantness.

Beard shaving off or taking off:
    losses of all kinds, multiple misfortunes

Beast, predacious animal:
beware of deceitful behaviour.

Beast, being beaten or attacked by one:
quarrel.

Bed, a beautiful one:
happiness and good harmony in your marriage.

Bed, not clean; uncomfortable:
unsociable, incompatible.

Bed of feathers/comforter or quilt, shaking, in sun:
family care.

Bed, burning:
disaster, illness, death.

Beds, rain falling onto:
excessiveness.

Bed, warmer, warm bottle:
soon to be married.

Bee, seeing:
always a good omen.

Bee, swarm:
confusing matters, complications.

Bee, being stung:
imminent bad luck, disagreements with friends.

Bees, very busy:
getting on, living well.

Bee honey, collecting honey from the combs:
passing on good advice.

Bees, gathered on a tree:
strengthening love and fidelity.

Bee hive, seeing:
delight and benefit.

Beef, cut up, seeing:
inheritance.

Beef, raw:
(see Meat)

Beer (blurry) drinking or seeing:
>   illness and annoyance.

Beer (clear) drinking or seeing:
>   steady health, cheerfulness and friendly meeting of people

Beer, spilling over:
>   declining wealth.

Beer-barrel:
>   business is taking off.

Beer-house, pub:
>   beware of carelessness.

Beet, turnip:
>   happy family, prosperity, luck in love.

Beet, field:
>   huge fortune ahead.

Beet-root, lots seeing:
>   getting into big ventures.

Beet-root, nice, a field:
>   development of your plans.

Beheaded, seeing yourself:
>   fear, affliction, loss of an influential sponsor.

Beheaded, seeing:
>   overcoming enemies, returning of a long missing friend.

Bell, seeing:
>   ventures with risk.

Bell-tower:
>   happiness, power, honour.

Bell, hearing one ring:
>   for business: good omen for contracts;
>   for married couple: arguments, disagreement.

Belly, big one:
>   being well-off, comfortable.

Belly, small:
>   long-lasting lawsuit.

Belly, swollen:
>   misfortune, hidden secrets.

Bellows:
> squabble, discord.

Belt, finding:
> gaining trust.

Belt, in silver:
> confined wealth.

Belt, losing:
> neglecting plans.

Belt, tearing apart:
> disaster.

Belt, new, wearing:
> forthcoming honour, soon to be engaged.

Bending down:
> degradation, harm.

Berries, eating or looking for:
> leadership and grief.

Bet, proposing and agreeing:
> uncertainty in business; losses ahead.

Betting:
> beware of risky speculation.

Bigger, becoming, seeing yourself growing huge:
> rich marriage.

Bile, vomiting:
> anger, annoyance.

Bill, accounting for:
> take good care of your documents.

Billiards, pool playing or seeing:
> doubtful venture inconsistency.

Binding, something:
> lawsuit matter.

Birds, singing:
> joy with your children, your loved ones seem happy.

Birds, flying:
> continuation in business, prosperous success.

Bird, in cage:
> secure assets.

Birds, colorful or strange, seeing:
> vulnerability where your friends are concerned.

Bird's nest, finding:
> experiencing plenty of joy.

Bird's nest, empty:
> annoyance, tricks.

Bird's nest, taking eggs from:
> grief and trouble in your daily life.

Birth (giving) seeing:
> difficulties, trouble.

Birth giving (a happy one), being present:
> joy, happiness.

Birth, giving, with complications, attending:
> losses, painful disgrace.

Birth, giving to a boy:
> prosperity in all undertakings.

Birth, giving to a girl:
> painful experiences at cheerfulness and joyfulness.

Bishop seeing:
> favoured by a dignitary.

Bite, to fear from an animal, or to escape from:
> jealousy.

Bleaching:
> illness.

Bleeding:
> falling into sadness.

Blessing, receiving:
> joy and happiness.

Blind, becoming:
> danger ahead.

Blind, being:
> being deceived by false friends.

Blind people, leading:
taking opportunities to help the needy.

Blind people, seeing:
interruption, obstacles in adventures.

Blinking-eye, seeing:
huge winnings.

Blisters, tearing with plaster (bandaid):
good health.

Block (log), hitting:
insult.

Blood, running from you:
good

Blood collecting, picking up:
good.

Blood drinking:
good.

Blood, rotten, foul:
severe illness.

Blood, being carried:
bad.

Blood collecting from an animal:
big business ambition.

Blood, seeing curdled:
illness.

Blood seeing of a nice color:
cheerfulness.

Blood, vomiting:
wealth for those who are poor.

Blueberries, eating:
scanty future ahead.

Boar, seeing:
being frightened; being followed by rivals.

Boar, seeing destroying crops:
dispute with friends.

Boar, hunt, shoot:
victory of a rival, overcoming danger.

Boar-wild, being attacked:
being held-up by evil people.

Boar, seeing one being killed:
freeing yourself from misery and fear.

Board-game, playing or seeing:
uncertainty and doubtful success in business deals.

Boarder, distinguishing and establishing:
money situation improving.

Boards, seeing:
flourishing business.

Boat, small:
forthcoming trip.

Boat, ferry, riding in, on sea or river, in clear water:
joy and success in all undertakings.

Boat sinking:
breakup of a love relationship.

Body deformation:
coming to shame.

Body, injuring:
trouble.

Body, your own, exposing:
falling into shame.

Bolt, seeing:
annoyance.

Bones, seeing:
lots of work ahead.

Bones, nibbling on:
food shortage.

Bonnet, putting on:
soon to be married.

Bonnet and hats, seeing:
lingering disease.

Boot, good and nice looking:
coming to honour, loyal servants.

Books buying:
being useful to yourself and others.

Books, learning from:
earning respect.

Books, seeing:
to gain through an unexpected event.

Books, seeing being burned:
hope for joy diminishing.

Books, useful ones, reading:
private speculation

Borrowing:
free yourself of worrisome matters.

Born, being:
needy person, good; well-off person, bad.

Bottles, broken:
sadness.

Bottles, cleaning:
being involved with bad company.

Bottle, seeing or having:
joy and fun.

Bottom (buttocks), seeing your own:
confusion in business.

Bottom, seeing of a woman:
succumb to trivial matters, or a silly fuss.

Bow, knot:
slipping into difficult involvement.

Bowl, dish:
dinner invitation.

Box, seeing:
discovering a secret.

Box, losing:
disagreement with yourself.

Box, in silver:
good omen.

Box, painted beautiful:
lots of fun.

Box, with a portrait:
soon a pleasant acquaintance.

Box-tree, shrub, seeing green:
firmness in your hopes.

Boys, seeing:
addition to the family.

Bracelets putting on:
secret love.

Bracelets, getting as a gift:
returning love.

Braided hair:
soon being united in love.

Branches, green:
your hopes are coming true.

Brandy, spirits, drinking or seeing:
evil lust.

Brass, merchandise, seeing:
being cheated.

Bread baking:
the undertakings are ending well.

Bread burned, seeing:
irresponsibility.

Bread eating:
having loyal friends and winning more.

Bread, eating while still warm:
becoming sick.

Bread seeing turning bad:
inconsistent luck.

Bread, being prepared:
for diligent people, good; lazy ones, bad.

Bread, seeing a nice loaf:
> to receive honour and wealth.

Bricklayer, seeing:
> laziness brings harm.

Breast, exposing:
> bashfulness, modesty.

Breast, big and healthy:
> enjoying sturdy health.

Breast, seeing, nursing a baby:
> joy in your marriage.

Breast, seeing a woman's:
> continuing to be in love.

Breast, hairy, seeing:
> lots of happiness in love.

Bride seeing, running:
> death.

Bride or groom, hugging:
> faithful, even at a far distance.

Bride or groom, escorting to the altar:
> peace of mind.

Bridge, weakening or driving over:
> happiness in love and all ventures.

Bridge, walking under:
> lots of obstacles but still reaching the goal.

Bridge, seeing:
> secure undertakings.

Bridge, seeing, being built of stone:
> durability in actions and proceedings.

Bridge, seeing, being built of wood:
> insupportable, destruction of hopes and actions.

Bridge, seeing, collapsing:
> big interruptions in business.

Bristles, seeing:
> there are obstacles in your ventures.

Broom:
> unpleasantness and difficulties among friends.

Brother or sister, talking or seeing:
> annoyance, disagreements.

Brother, seeing him walk off with death (image):
> diminishing of a powerful enemy.

Brother, saying farewell to him:
> sadness, depression.

Broth, drinking or eating:
> good proceedings in business; ill-person, slow recovery; lovers will soon tie the knot.

Broken pieces:
> all earthly things are transient.

Brushing:
> lots of fun.

Buck, rammler killing:
> defeat of enemies.

Buckle:
> continuation in business ventures.

Building, seeing one being demolished:
> brushing obstacles aside.

Building, nice and large:
> ventures, undertakings.

Building, small living in:
> peace of mind with your destiny.

Buffalo, seeing:
> big casualties, losses.

Bull, seeing or being pursued:
> risk, loosing a dear friend, unpleasantness from family members.

Bullet, being hit:
> you will need a doctor's care.

Bullets, rolling in front of you:
> ill-fated success.

Bullets, flying into your house:
> danger lies ahead.

Bumps on your body, swollen:
> getting real estate.

Burden, heavy:
> depression.

Burdock sticking on you:
> warning of obtrusive people.

Buried, being yourself, seeing:
> health and long life.

Buried being alive:
> coming into great danger.

Burial watching:
> sorrow, discord, illness or disease.

Burning, seeing:
> forthcoming disaster.

Burning glass, looking through:
> error, mistake.

Bushes, cutting up:
> removing all obstacles out of love.

Bushes (underbrush), seeing:
> expect obstacles.

Bushes, hiding behind:
> danger at present.

Businessman, seeing:
> good progress in ventures.

Butcher, seeing or talking:
> being offended, loosing your lover, rejection.

Butter, eating:
> discord, conflict, annoyance with relatives.

Butter, making:
> inner calmness.

Butterfly, seeing or catching:
> unsteadiness, unfaithfulness.

Buying something:
> wasting brings disadvantage.

Cabbage, seeing, being eaten:
   unexpected grief, sorrow.

Cabbage leaves, Savoy, eating or seeing:
   pretending happiness, showing off.

Cabinet-maker or cabinet-makers, shop visiting:
   messed up matters, cleaning up.

Cage, cleaning out:
   imprisonment, or other danger.

Cage, emptying of birds:
   release of affliction.

Cake (torte), fancy:
   rivalry is harming your health.

Cake, baking:
   happiness, prosperity.

Calculate, without reading a result:
   annoyance, cheating.

Calendar, seeing:
   achieving a better living standard.

Calves, seeing:
   unwise tricks.

Calves, being killed:
   recovery from illness.

Camel, seeing:
   experiencing something out of the ordinary, becoming rich.

Can (jug):
   good news.

Can (jug), drinking from:
   joy.

Can (watering):
   (see watering can).

Canary, seeing or hearing:
   empty compliments.

Candlelight:
being spared trouble.

Candles, seeing:
invitation to a happy occasion.

Candles, blowing out:
giving up an acquaintance.

Candles, burning, carrying:
death.

Cannon ball, seeing:
sorrow

Cannon discharge:
withstanding something repulsive

Canopy, seeing:
a position of dignity, joy

Canteen, woman, talking or seeing:
late, but not too late, coming out of misery.

Car, flipping one over:
relief from worries.

Cardinal:
happiness and welfare.

Card player, seeing:
escaping from danger.

Card playing:
arguments, unhappy in your love, late marriage.

Card playing, with lots of pictures in it:
favourable prospects, rich bride

Card playing, with lots of hearts in it:
happy, satisfying marriage and many children.

Card tricks:
seeking popularity.

Cargo-wagon:
busy activity in your business.

Carnations:
your descendants bring you lots of joy.

Carp, eating or seeing:
   health improvement.

Carpets:
   fondness of luxury and waste brings decline in prosperity.

Carrier-seeing:
   anger, discord.

Carrion-animal:
   good times, long life.

Case (box), seeing or owing:
   stolen goods are being returned.

Cash box, yours, or seeing one:
   disadvantage in business.

Cast - wheelbarrow, pulling:
   live beyond one's means.

Castle, seeing:
   very good, joyful, omen.

Castle on fire:
   disaster, illness.

Cattle, seeing:
   virtuous acquaintances or engagement.

Cattle, guiding:
   immediately, prosperity, then bad luck

Cats seeing:
   annoyance, persecution, cheated by lover, or servants,
   having contact with false people, and not knowing it.

Cats, being scratched or bitten by:
   coming into evil care taking.

Catching:
   insidiousness.

Caterpillar:
   damage to your belongings.

Cauliflower:
   honour.

Cave, dying in it:
   low in spirit, depression.

Caves, seeing or living in:
big changes in your luck and happiness.

Celery:
beware of flattery.

Cellar, seeing or being in:
sickness lies ahead.

Cellar, sweeping:
bad business.

Cellar steps, falling down:
prolonging disease.

Chain, seeing:
imprisonment, pursuit outwitted by enemies, soon taking
your bride to the altar.

Chain, wearing:
bad, disastrous times ahead.

Chain, being chained:
a position is being offered.

Chair, beautiful, seeing:
promotion, high position, wealth.

Chair, dirty and worn out:
interruption or destroying family harmony.

Chair of many colours:
happy times ahead.

Chair in black, seeing:
death.

Chair, sitting in it:
unstable health.

Chalk:
you will lose a lot of money.

Chamomile:
you will live to an old age.

Chandelier:
festivities lie ahead.

Chapel, seeing:
joy and loyal friends.

Chaplain, becoming:
 great honour.

Charity, receiving:
 Changing luck.

Charm, being charmed or fascinated:
 losing business deals.

Charming someone:
 becoming imprudent.

Chasm, seeing, falling into, being swallowed by:
 fast rescue from danger.

Charity, handing out:
 deep gratitude, calmness, satisfaction.

Cheek:
 take more care about cleanness.

Cheeks, scratched and skinny:
 sadness and sorrow.

Cheeks, big and red:
 good prospect.

Cherry tree:
 nice weather.

Cherries, eating or seeing:
 awkwardness in many things.

Cherries, sour, eating:
 depression, sorrow.

Cheese, eating or seeing:
 happiness and health.

Chess game:
 overall knowledge is the best investments.

Chest (box), empty:
 annoyance, misfortune.

Chest (box), filled:
 plenty.

Chest, being wounded:
 for seniors, a bad omen; for youth, a good omen.

Children falling down:
> disruptions, and often decline in business venture.

Children, seeing:
> joy, health, happiness, inner peace, happy marriage, success in all undertakings.

Children at play:
> joyfulness, cheerfulness, peace of mind.

Childbirth:
> addition to the family, increasing prosperity.

Chimney:
> good family life.

Chimney sweep:
> rescue from danger.

China (dishes):
> thirst for pleasure is wasting your life away.

Chives:
> trouble, damage at your undertakings.

Choking:
> you will soon be well.

Christ, worshipping:
> joy.

Christ, seeing on the cross:
> perish.

Christ, hearing him speak:
> joyfulness.

Church, seeing:
> protection from evil and bad things to come.

Church, praying in it:
> happiness, joyfulness, progress in all good things.

Church destroyed, or seeing in ruin:
> forthcoming disaster.

Churchyard, seeing:
> disease.

Cigar, making:
> health.

Cigar smoking:
enjoyment and wealth.

Circle:
punctuality in office brings sure profit in business.

City hall:
involvement in lawsuits.

City, large, walking through it:
vexation of all kinds, restlessness.

City, small and friendly, seeing:
frugality, making a good living.

City, with many high towers:
starting a grand operation, enterprise.

City, seeing destroyed:
misfortune, loss of honour and wealth.

Clergyman, seeing or talking:
comforting, for the sick or lovers of bad consequences.

Cliff, seeing:
your calculation is wrong.

Climbing up a hill:
repulsiveness.

Climbing a tree:
obtaining honour, dignity, long courtship.

Climbing a mast:
poverty and affliction.

Clock, seeing:
being aware of the presence.

Clothing, shabby, wearing:
poverty.

Closet, seeing:
sincerity is more pleasing than being reserved.

Clouds, condensed, like a mountain:
to my regret.

Clouds, black and heavy:
discord, arguments, misery.

Clover, seeing being planted:
happy family life.

Clover, four-leafed, finding:
extraordinary luck.

Clover field, lush and green:
hopeful future.

Clyster, seeing:
your business is proceeding well.

Clyster, getting:
riches, wealth.

Clucking (hen), seeing:
luck and blessings.

Coach (carriage), riding in it:
tendency to haughtiness, sure downfall, misery.

Coach (carriage), stepping out:
losing trust and respectful position.

Coal, seeing:
great wealth, luck.

Coal, seeing burning:
be careful in choosing friends, all in all, carefulness.

Coal, wanted to eat:
misfortune, bad luck.

Coalmine:
marrying a widow.

Coat of Arms:
haughtiness.

Coat, new, putting on:
termination of previous worries.

Coat, too big, putting on:
grief, sadness.

Coat, wearing, or seeing:
dignity.

Coat, tearing:
separation.

Coat, losing:
> forthcoming misery.

Coat, animal skin, tanner:
> everybody is mad.

Cock (chafer):
> distrust, causing suspicion.

Cockade, seeing or wearing:
> courage, dignified behaviour.

Cockade, not yours, wearing:
> treason and ingratitude.

Cook, seeing:
> unnecessary expenses.

Cookies, eating:
> means, good times ahead.

Cooking:
> a fun and cheerful festivity lies ahead.

Coffee, seeing or roasting:
> misfortune, bad luck, persecution.

Coffee grinding:
> annoyance, trouble.

Coffee house, being in it:
> accident of a friend or relative.

Coffin, seeing:
> a long and happy life.

Coins, precious metal:
> considerable riches, lucky business deals.

Colonnade, seeing, touring, walking:
> riches, happiness.

Colic, having:
> sickness in the family.

Color, paint in a box:
> full cash register.

Column (pillar) seeing:
> coming to honour.

Column (pillar), collapsing:
becoming an invalid; illness.

Comb:
Illness and worries.

Combing hair:
effortless work.

Comedy (play):
contempt, blasphemy.

Comet, seeing:
price hikes, war, dying and torment, bad harvest, unexpected news.

Comfort, receiving and not needing it:
good.

Communion (holy) receiving:
steady happiness, finding friends in troublesome times.

Company (get together) in horse-back riding or driving:
tendency for waste and extravagance.

Concert, attending:
grief, loss of relatives and friends.

Confectionery (sweets), eating:
advantage, benefit.

Conference room, court room, attending a public meeting:
being in pursuit of political activities.

Confessional:
many disagreeable people.

Confessional (priest), church clerk, seeing or confessing to:
confused in business.

Conquest in war:
authority, prestige and honour.

Contrabass, seeing:
dispute, arguments.

Contrabass being played:
unity, harmony.

Convertible (car) driving:
joy and happiness.

Copper (money):
 effortless work.

Cord (chain), of gold, seeing:
 profit, remarkable improvement of your assets.

Coronation of a King or Queen, attending:
 prosperous success at present, favorable situation.

Corset (undergarment):
 vanity brings deep sorrow.

Corpse being buried:
 lovers soon to be separated.

Corpse, seeing:
 wedding.

Corpulence:
 increasing your wealth.

Cotton, waving:
 gain, profit.

Cotton shrub:
 riches, wealth.

Coughing:
 your secrets are being revealed.

Counterfeiting:
 shame, disgrace, misery.

Court, being prosecuted:
 confusion, perplexity.

Courthouse, standing in front of one:
 seeking your rights.

Courtroom:
 bad luck, repulsiveness.

Cover, seeking from enemies:
 fraud.

Cows, seeing
 success in ventures.

Cow milk, drinking:
 unstable health.

Cow stable, being in it:
 relieved from an illness.

Cowl, seeing:
 peace of mind, state of bliss.

Crab, eating or seeing:
 declining business, pain, disagreement.

Cradle, seeing:
 bright future.

Crane (bird), seeing:
 bad omen, disaster, disloyal friends or servants.

Cranes (birds), flying:
 good news.

Cranes (birds) crying:
 joy.

Creditor, seeing or being visited by:
 secure, but effortless business.

Creek, with many fish:
 good inheritance.

Creek, with blood flowing:
 illness caused by blood vomiting.

Creek, dried out:
 poverty, lingering prolonging illness.

Creek, clear, seeing running into your house:
 means increase of fortune and wealth.

Creek, muddy, seeing running into your house:
 illness, grief, sadness.

Creek, swelling, rising of water level:
 growing assets, also fast declining of such.

Crescent, seeing:
 secured food supply.

Crib, seeing empty:
 bad paid work.

Crib, filled:
 huge profit.

Criminal (person), seeing:
    disagreeable people.

Crippled person:
    unexpected help.

Crocodile, seeing:
    a warning about false people around you.

Crop (Goiter), on you, or seeing on others:
    excessiveness makes you sick.

Crop (harvest), yellow without spikes:
    your plans to succeed.

Crop (harvest), beautifully green:
    big hopes for a soon acquisition.

Cross (holy), decorated with flowers:
    happy family life.

Cross (holy), seeing:
    sorrow.

Cross (holy), on your head:
    defamation.

Crossbow, stretching:
    fear and trouble.

Crossbow, breaking:
    good future.

Crow (bird), crying:
    receiving bad news.

Crow (birds), many on a tree:
    a get-together of relatives.

Crow (bird), seeing:
    death.

Crown, seeing or wearing:
    wealth and honour.

Crown of myrtle, seeing or wearing:
    invitation to a wedding, or your own wedding.

Crowned, being:
    sadness.

Cruelty, abuse:
    insult.

Crust (scab), on the head:
    acquisition of great wealth.

Crutches, using:
    losing your lover, clumsiness in undertakings.

Crutches seeing, being used by others:
    getting help, support from unknown friends.

Cuckoo, seeing or crying:
    joy and good health.

Cucumber, eating, or seeing:
    illness.

Cuffs, on sleeves, wearing:
    coming to honour.

Cuffs, on sleeves, of lace:
    privilege.

Cuffs, on sleeves, dirty or with holes:
    losing your job.

Cups (mugs), seeing:
    being surprised by an unexpected visitor.

Cup (mug), breaking:
    death of an enemy.

Cup, made of silver:
    profit, gain.

Cup, letting it fall:
    nervousness, anxiety.

Cup, a nice painted one, breaking:
    imminent misfortune.

Cup (goblet), drinking from it:
    good times ahead.

Currant (red berry), eating or seeing:
    steadfast, perseverance.

Currant (white berry):
    satisfaction.

Currant (berry), seeing or eating:
  stability in love.

Currant (berry) black:
  unfaithfulness

Curl (ringlet):
  true love.

Curtain:
  discovering a secret.

Customs building:
  beware of cheaters.

Cypress tree, seeing:
  sadness, declining in business.

Dagger, losing:
  poverty.

Dagger, holding in your hands:
  joy and honour.

Dagger, hitting a stranger:
  luck in business.

Dagger, and bloodshed, seeing:
  having secret sponsors.

Dagger, feeling danger to life:
  swamped with charities.

Dagger, receiving from a dignitary:
  great honour.

Dagger, seeing broken:
  death, disease.

Dagger, seeing:
  news from friends.

Dagger, pursuing a person:
  victory over your enemies.

Dagger, being hurt by:
  favors from friends.

Dairy, visiting:
being happy in your occupation, getting rich, or receiving honour, on trips happy times.

Dam, working on it:
good progress in your project.

Dancing:
unexpected good news from a distant friend.

Dancing and falling:
humiliation, arrogance.

Darkness, finding the way to the light:
rescue from great danger.

Darkness, being in it:
misery, difficulty.

Dates, giving away:
you will be kissed.

Dates, eating:
being favoured by a woman.

Daw, flying:
very bad news.

Dawn - rosy, seeing:
stormy days ahead.

Dead, seeing yourself:
joy.

Dead, being and coming back to life again:
honour and happy news.

Dead, seeing a friend:
receiving news from an estranged friend.

Dead, people, seeing:
abused by friends, losing your lover, losing on a horse deal.

Dead, bodies, digging up:
experiencing cruelty.

Dead, bodies, on a battlefield:
sorrow lies ahead.

Dead, body with wreath, seeing:
lingering illness.

Dead person, seeing, eating with him/her:
  great honour.

Dead people, seeing awakening:
  dispute about inheritance.

Dead, being dead:
  late marriage, luck in ventures.

Death - bier death bed:
  unexpected inheritance.

Debt, paying off:
  grief, worries.

Deer, seeing:
  pursuing someone innocent.

Deer, seeing running:
  means quick start in your trade

Deer, shooting:
  inheritance, honour, humiliating weak and fearful enemies.

Deer herd, seeing:
  many friendships.

Deer hind, seeing:
  wealth, prosperity and happiness.

Dentist, seeing or talking to:
  fraud and misfortune.

Denuding yourself:
  experiencing shame.

Deprived, being:
  losing a relative.

Desertion from your faith:
  bad business deals, ruin.

Despair:
  hardship, repulsiveness.

Devil, seeing:
  bad luck, interruption in plans, tricked by false people.

Diadem, putting on:
  losses, insults, offence.

Diamonds, seeing:
false luck.

Diamonds, receiving:
annoyance, bad luck.

Diamonds, eating:
happiness, reward, advantage.

Diarrhea:
health.

Dice:
hostility, disagreeableness.

Dice, playing:
happy event, marrying chosen partner, wealth, honour.

Dinner, being invited:
you are well respected.

Dinner, smelling burned:
unpleasant news.

Dirt:
damage through slander.

Dirty, being:
illness.

Dirty, making yourself:
happiness.

Dishes, of metal:
good marriage, or satisfaction.

Dishes, breaking:
brawl, dispute, feud.

Dishes, seeing:
domestic twist, disagreement.

Dispute, getting involved:
anxiety, fear.

Distill - cork, seeing:
annoyance, trouble.

Ditch, falling into:
caution about traps, falseness.

Ditch, jumping over:
treason, unfaithfulness.

Ditch, standing before a deep one:
danger.

Doctor, seeing one who bandaged a relative:
impending marriage in the family.

Doctor, seeing with patient, having a friendly talk:
impending indisposition.

Doctor, visits you:
privilege and happiness.

Doctor, seeing:
for a sick person, health; for a healthy person, death.

Documents, receiving:
promotion.

Dog, white, seeing:
pleasant acquaintance.

Dog, being attacked by:
approaching danger.

Dogs being chased:
unsteadiness, excess.

Dogs, fighting:
family discord about inheritance.

Dog house:
decline in your social status.

Dogs, owning one yourself:
great wealth.

Dogs at play:
luck in business, reconciliation with those on bad terms, winning back estranged friends, truly being loved again.

Dolphin, playing:
misfortune or even death.

Domestic (servants):
lots of effort and work.

Donation, handing out:
piece of mind, satisfaction.

Donations, receiving:
    change of luck.

Donkey, buying:
    economy, gain.

Donkey, crying:
    losses, damage and struggle.

Donkey, hitting:
    hard-hearted towards your loved ones.

Donkey, loaded with baggage:
    gain of wealth, prosperous ventures, much respect.

Donkey, riding on:
    slowly but surely reaching your goal.

Donkey, seeing:
    in love, loyalty and obligingness, prosperous business.

Door, burning or destroyed, seeing:
    dying friends or relative.

Dove:
    pleasant news.

Dove, catching:
    annoyance.

Dove cote:
    peace and harmony.

Doves flying:
    good news, luck in business.

Drag, seeing:
    many obstacles in your ventures.

Dragon, flying:
    false happiness.

Draw bridge:
    unexpected trip.

Drawing (sketch):
    truthful friends.

Dress closet:
    luck and profit.

Dress fabric, seeing:
vanity causes heartbreak.

Dress, having a beautiful one:
coming into good circumstances.

Dress, putting one on:
luck, good circumstances.

Dress, white:
luck in love and all ventures.

Dresses, black:
sorrow, losing your lover, painful experiences.

Dresses, blue or purple:
happiness, joy, prosperity, loyal friends.

Dresses, colorful, seeing:
changing luck, annoyance by your lover, danger to lose
them, inconsistency in affections.

Dresses, crimson:
old age, honour, your love was a happy choice.

Dresses , dark red:
losing suspicious friends, quarrelling about pedantry,
annoyance from your children.

Dresses, dirty, torn:
difficulties in marrying the girl you've chosen, losing friends.

Dresses, from other nations, seeing:
long trip ahead.

Dresses, green:
priority from your lover or suitor, or preferred offers.

Dresses, yellow:
falseness, jealousy, losing people who meant well.

Dresses, tearing apart:
annoyance ahead, anger.

Dresses, washing:
becoming economical, saving.

Dressing gown, wearing:
indisposition experiencing.

Drink, given to you:
invitation will be received.

Drink, mixing:
> imminent sickness in the family.

Drinking glasses, decorative:
> getting out of a bad situation.

Drinking fresh water:
> good omen.

Drinking from a glass:
> risk, revealing secrets.

Drinking vinegar:
> discord, dissension of family members.

Drinks:
> be careful of your enemies.

Driving and turning over:
> forthcoming accident.

Driving, seeing:
> envy, jealousy.

Driving, in a car or carriage to a wedding or baby christening:
> to have honour and power, especially when a carriage is being pulled by people, and you don't get hurt.

Drowning:
> prosperity and happiness.

Drowning, witnessing:
> triumph, victory over your enemies.

Drowned, being:
> losses of all kinds.

Drum (drummer):
> enduring small losses.

Drunk, being:
> will entertain unexpected and unknown friends.

Drunk people, seeing:
> repulsiveness, abhorrence.

Drunkenness, being addicted:
> happiness and health.

Duck, beautiful, seeing:
> great honour, for our slanders it means losses and sorrow.

Ducks, catching:
success in receiving approval or acceptance.

Ducks, trying to catch:
casualties.

Ducks, swimming:
overcoming bad gossip.

Ducks, wild geese, flying:
joyful message.

Duel, participating in:
impending danger of death.

Dumb person, seeing:
charity brings blessings.

Dumplings, eating or making:
gossip will bring harm.

Dwarf (gnome):
being persuaded by weak enemies.

Dying:
receiving many empty promises.

Eagle (owl):
beware of wrongful company.

Eagle, your own:
strength in your intention.

Eagle, flying high in circles:
prosperity, wealth, honour, happiness in love.

Eagle, sitting on your head:
a death.

Eagle, standing or sitting on you:
for rich person, death; for poor person, goodness.

Earth, talking to:
very good, huge wealth and prosperity.

Earth, seeing split apart:
forthcoming danger.

Earthquake, feeling:
changes, uncertainty, unstable future.

Earth (soil), black:
annoyance, misfortune, affliction.

Earth (soil; ground), yellow or glowing:
happiness, success, loyal friendship

Earth (soil), being worked:
family growth.

Earthworms, seeing:
influential, powerful enemies.

Ears, beautiful or extremely large:
seeing a friend happy.

Ears, pulled:
unfair treatment, suppressed hopes.

Ears, like a donkey:
being abused.

Ears, cleaning:
loyal servants.

Earrings, wearing or seeing:
treason, effortless work.

Eating, seeing others:
invitation.

Eating, yourself:
difficulties with your loved ones, misfortune in business, annoyance in love, arguments and trouble.

Eclipse:
losing many friends through defamation, getting a bad reputation.

Eel, removing from water:
for the sick, health; for the healthy, goodness.

Eel, seeing stripped down:
for a prisoner, freedom; for others, help from misery.

Eel, seeing dead:
sorrow and annoyance.

Eggs, belonging to you:
gain, harmony in the family.

Eggs, broken:
losses, arguments, poverty, separation from friends or lover.

Eggs, eating:
becoming a father, happiness.

Eggs, dropping:
disharmony

Eggs, finding:
becoming a bride or groom.

Eggs, opening, rotten:
bad reputation.

Eggs, red, seeing:
anger, fire, death of a friend.

Eggs, seeing or buying:
good success in business, improving prosperity, promotion, good children, old age.

Eggs, seeing yellow:
serious illness.

Elder (bush):
recovery from an old, lingering health problem.

Elephant, seeing, being killed:
destroying of plans.

Elephant, killed by you:
death.

Elephant, seeing:
big plans, luck in business deals, late but good marriage.

Embroider (embroidery):
reaching for the unthinkable, being a slave in awe.

Emperor and kings, seeing:
lots of luck.

Endive, or other greens, eating:
difficulties.

Enema, seeing:
impenetrable business.

Enemy, meeting:
overcoming unpleasantness, defeating rival, strengthening your position, overcoming all troubles.

Engagement:
 growing family.

Engagement time:
 reverence, veneration, worship.

Englishman, seeing or talking to:
 false friends, bad creditors.

Entertainment (amusement):
 losses.

Ermine, putting on, wearing:
 happiness and great wealth.

Escape, helping:
 because of your goodness, inconvenience, trouble and difficulties.

Escaping:
 avoiding danger.

Essences (perfume), using:
 unfaithfulness, being cheated in general.

Estate, inheriting:
 becoming a bride or groom.

Estate, buying:
 return of being well-off.

Estate, selling:
 decline in economic activity.

Estate owning, a beautiful one:
 ability to have peace.

Estate, countryside, getting:
 unexpected inheritance.

Estate, country, cultivating:
 activity.

Evergreen, seeing or picking:
 loyal friendship.

Execution, witnessing:
 dubious success in ventures.

Execution, place, going to or seeing:
 happiness and honour.

Executioner, seeing:
expulsion.

Exile, being sent:
great love; for an ill person, health

Exile, received as a judgement:
changing the views about business.

Eyebrows, falling out:
disaster.

Eyebrows seeing, black:
health.

Eyelids, big and beautiful:
honour and respect.

Eyeglasses, your own, wearing:
becoming vain, being laughed at, being fooled.

Eyeglasses, sunglasses, wearing:
caution about friends.

Eyes, bad, weak:
losses of all sorts, short on money.

Eyes, being robbed of them:
shattered hopes, losing a good friend, unpleasantness in love.

Eyes, beautiful, your own:
happiness and riches.

Eyes, good vision:
you have good people around you.

Eyes, squinting:
humiliating yourself.

Eyes, watering:
bad future, losing your good reputation.

Fabric (garment), buying or seeing:
lucky projects.

Face, covering:
bad, serious news

Face, refined in mirror, seeing:
 your wishes being fulfilled.

Face, your own, beautiful:
 proceedings in your projects and plans.

Face, your own, ugly, seeing:
 many worries, sorrow.

Face, ugly, seeing in water:
 enmity, hostility.

Face, beautiful, seeing in water:
 long life.

Face, meeting a beautiful one:
 much joy.

Face, pale:
 illness, death.

Face, putting makeup on:
 for a woman who doesn't need it, good; for a man, mockery and contempt.

Face, without a nose:
 death.

Face washing:
 remorse, repentance.

Factory (company), owning or seeing:
 flourishing business.

Fair (market):
 communication with many people.

Fainting:
 unpleasant news.

Fairy, seeing or talking to:
 much luck and happiness in all matters of life.

Falcon, golden:
 honour.

Falcon, flying:
 being cheated.

Falling from a high place:
disaster, loss of honour and respect, and your fortune.

Falling, but holding on:
to be saved or protected from bad luck.

Falling over an obstacle:
getting information.

Falling and being hurt:
many conflicts.

Fan, hand held:
betrayal.

Farewell:
loyalty, friendship.

Farmer, seeing:
luck, happiness.

Farmyard:
rich inheritance.

Fat, eating:
illness.

Fat (stout) being:
means unexpected wealth.

Fat (oil), cooking:
losses.

Fat, plump children, your own:
good years are ahead.

Father, becoming:
worrisome, but good times experiencing.

Father, of many children:
increasing worries.

Feast, attending:
unpleasantness, worries, discord in love, annoyance from children.

Feathers, being covered:
interruptions in business.

Feathers, black seeing:
recession in business, annoyance.

Feathers, taking:
honour.

Feathers, white, owning:
being cleared from false suspicions.

Feather quill, writing:
good news.

Feathers, white, seeing:
welfare and amusement.

Feathers, seeing many flying:
hoped for luck in vain.

Feeding animals:
good progress in projects.

Feet, breaking:
receiving pity, because of an accident.

Feet, deformed:
ignorance.

Feet, dirty:
nasty sickness ahead.

Feet, seeing, not attached to a body:
imminent, soon danger.

Feet, sore:
finding support for your business.

Feet, washing:
falling ill, suffering.

Fence:
others want you in chains, handcuffs, to restrain you.

Festivities, attending:
painful news of sorrow.

Fever having:
unsteady love and friendship.

Fever, seeing others being affected:
happiness in marriage, peace of mind without wealth.

Field, green and beautiful:
> hope of a good occupation, happy in love and marriage, wealth and honour in prospect of prosperous position.

Field, uncultivated:
> stagnant plans.

Field, working over:
> activity.

Field, lay waste:
> sadness.

Field, destroyed by hail:
> false speculation

Field, in beautiful bloom:
> success of your hopes.

Field, running through it, or on horseback:
> soon receiving message from the person you await.

Field, planting and sowing:
> for those courting a woman and want children, good; for others, work, illness and displeasure.

Fig, eating or seeing:
> happiness in marriage and love.

Fig, receiving as a gift:
> friendly behaviour.

Fig tree, seeing:
> being shielded, protected.

Fight (battle):
> seduction.

Fighting:
> dispute, argument.

Fighting on horseback:
> getting a rich woman from a good family.

Fighting with wild animals and defeat:
> being rescued from great danger.

Fighting:
> frustration about your hopes, separation or loss of lover.

Fighting and prize-winning:
> happy ending to started ventures.

File (office), receiving:
warning or information about enemies.

Finding money or other things:
your worries will soon be lifted.

Fine, paying:
advantage.

Finger, burned:
falling into temptation.

Finger, cut and bleeding:
luck in love.

Finger, losing:
indicates damage.

Finger, very nice, seeing:
respect and honour.

Fingernails, long and nice:
wealth, honour, a good wife, unexpected money.

Finger ring, losing or giving away:
suffering and lingering illness.

Finger ring, receiving:
great honour.

Fire (blaze), seeing:
unconditional love, wealth, your children are being blessed.

Fire, blowing out:
abandon projects and plans.

Fire engine:
danger lies ahead.

Fire engines, driving fast:
imminent misfortune.

Fire, falling from sky:
experiencing hardship.

Fire, falling into:
great losses, ill humour.

Fire, bright flames, burning one or more buildings:
forthcoming honour, much goodness.

Fire, huge, seeing houses diminish in smoke and ashes:
disaster of all kinds, first at family members.

Fire, losing:
bad omen.

Fire, seeing it go out on stove:
for sick person, death.

Fire, small, on your stove:
riches, wealth.

Fire, running over it:
annoyance.

Fire, running away from it:
vexation ahead.

Fire, pail:
forthcoming danger.

Fire, burning bright:
being loved and not knowing it.

Fire, lighting, but not burning:
not being loved.

Fire, signs, seeing in the sky:
rising cost of living, enemy invasion, much misery.

Fireworks, seeing:
happiness

Fish, catching:
negligence

Fish, big, buying or seeing:
luck and advantage.

Fish, seeing:
bad profit, sadness, illness, annoyance.

Fish, eating, fried:
forthcoming prosperity.

Fish, seeing being sold:
unpleasant entertainment

Fish, small, buying or eating:
losses of all kind.

Fish, slippery, seeing:
a hope for profit diminishes, or unfaithfulness.

Fish, receiving as a gift:
being swamped with fake honours.

Fish pond:
avoid sloppiness and dirtiness.

Fishing gear, tackle, seeing:
fraud, persecution.

Flag, carrying:
you will be honoured.

Flag, flying in the wind:
danger, bad luck ahead.

Flames, clear and bright, seeing:
receiving money, or jewelry as a gift.

Flax, beautiful, seeing:
savings in the household budget.

Flax, spin to nice threats:
finding good accommodation.

Flattering, caress:
evil meaning.

Fleas, on you:
overcoming your enemies.

Fleas, seeing many, being bitten:
misfortune, poverty, difficulties.

Fleet, naval, full sails:
imminent changes.

Flies (insects), seeing many:
having enemies, being stalked, grief and insult.

Flies, killing:
hostility, all in all to get rid of unpleasant things.

Flying and falling:
inconvenience.

Flying, long distance:
pleasant days ahead, luck in ventures, praise.

Flying towards heaven:
for servants, good; for others, a trip; for the sick, death.

Flying, from a high perch:
arrogance.

Flood, high tide, seeing:
with people around you, or family, disagreements.

Flood, seeing:
losses of all kinds.

Floor, in different patterns, seeing, or walking on:
sorrow and joy.

Flour, seeing:
case of death.

Flour, roasting:
unexpected misfortune.

Flower bucket:
joy, instantaneous satisfaction.

Flowers, beautiful:
much joy.

Flowers, receiving as a gift:
honourable days.

Flowers, picking and binding together:
soon to be engaged.

Flowers, planting:
performing an act of kindness.

Flowers, scattered:
negligence, recklessness.

Flowers, tearing up:.
spoiling your happiness, luck.

Flute, playing:
disagreements, losses.

Fog:
(see Mist).

Fools, seeing, or talking:
being cheated.

Foolish, being crazy:
remarkable success in business.

Foolishness, craziness by friends or loved ones:
reconciliation with enemy, attachment, great mentors.

Foot bridge, over water:
being frightened.

Foot path, narrow, walking:
don't leave the path of virtues, the only way to happiness.

Forehead, high and wide:
indicates that you are using your head, concerns about decisions in your business.

Forehead, narrow and small:
you must show courage.

Forehead, wounded:
treason, finding out about it.

Forest, seeing:
a pleasant winter lies ahead.

Forest, seeing, walking through, logging:
happy marriage, peace of mind, getting a fortune.

Forest, on fire:
enduring great losses.

Forest, walking in with great effort, endlessly:
defamation, pursuit, deceived by friends.

Forester's house:
being well-accepted on a trip.

Forest ranger, meeting:
imminent mischief.

Forge (iron), seeing:
getting plenty of work.

Forge, hammer, hearing:
you will hear something pleasant.

Forget-me-not, flowers:
you will be well remembered.

Fork, seeing:
being deceived.

Fortress, seeing:
>	unexpected opposition, hostility, also illness.

Fortress, (ruins) seeing:
>	sadness.

Fortress (ruins), climbing on:
>	fearless in any danger.

Fortress ruins, falling down from it:
>	being harmed.

Fortress, under fire:
>	war times.

Fountain, seeing:
>	a merry festivity ahead.

Fox, chasing or killing:
>	getting to know false friends and their tricky intentions.

Foxes, creeping, crawling:
>	secret enemies thinking of bringing you down.

French horn, musical instruments, seeing:
>	pleasant news.

Friend, seeing deceased:
>	unexpected novelty news, postponing marriage.

Friend seeing, welcoming:
>	to reach fame and honour.

Friends, insulting:
>	disdain.

Friends, joking around:
>	separation.

Frighten, terrifying:
>	danger, bad luck.

Frills, ruffles, seeing:
>	vanity gets you in deep affliction or sorrow.

Frogs, seeing in pond:
>	plenty of money, lucky business, loyal love, married
>	couple blessed with children, pleasant company on trips.

Frogs, catching or killing:
>	suicide, harming yourself.

Frogs, hearing them croak:
praise and fame.

Frostbite:
carefulness in all activities.

Fruit, giving away:
finding mentors and friends.

Fruit in baskets, seeing in storage:
good omen.

Fruit tree:
good continuation in your new business.

Fruit, seeing:
beware of opponents, forthcoming unpleasantness.

Fruit, sour, eating or seeing:
misfortune and illness.

Fruit, sweet, eating or seeing:
great fortune, happiness.

Frying pan, seeing:
harm, injury.

Fryingspit, rotating:
bad luck and pursuit.

Funeral, attending:
late marriage, mishap or death of a friend or relative.

Funeral, arranging:
for married couple, family additions; for single person,
impending marriage; for servants, pomotion.

Funeral, procession, seeing:
unexpected inheritance

Funnel:
don't reach for the unattainable.

Fur, receiving as a gift:
getting to know many mentors.

Fur, seeing:
progress in your occupation, trade.

Fur, wearing:
gaining respect.

Fury, bewitched people:
anger, rage, hate, enmity.

Gable, seeing collapse:
accident, death.

Gall-nut, oak apple, eating or finding:
culminate, slander.

Galley (slave):
courage, boldness.

Gallows, seeing:
false friends, misfortune, unrest.

Gallows, going to be hanged:
coming to honour.

Game of forfeits:
distraction is a disadvantage to your business.

Game (venison):
war, starvation, discord by lovers, dishonest friends.

Game (venison) meat eating:
prosperity.

Gamble (money):
quarrel, dispute.

Garden, neglected, disorganized:
being surrounded by false advisors.

Garden, beautiful landscaped, walking through:
enjoying amusements, growth of investments,
forthcoming honour, good projects.

Garden, high-fenced, seeing:
denial of request.

Garlic smell:
repulsiveness, adversity.

Garment, buying:
happiness.

Garter, wearing or seeing:
bad luck, annoyance.

Gate, seeing open:
your visitors are welcome.

Gauze, on hat or arm, wearing:
means sad, mournful message.

Gazebo with Jasmine flowers:
engagement.

Geese, seeing flying:
losses.

Geese, seeing:
happiness, great wealth, absent friends seeing soon.

Geese, killing:
little pity for the needy.

Gem, seeing:
falling into temptation.

Gem, your own:
attain great honour.

Gem, receiving:
increasing your wealth.

Gem, wearing:
arrogance.

Ghost, seeing:
temptation to sin, danger, losing lover or friend, news of a
death.

Giant, seeing:
good omen, success in business.

Gift, giving:
forthcoming new and honest friends.

Gift, receiving:
dealing with difficulties.

Gingerbread, eating:
innocent joy.

Gypsy:
beware of irresponsible tricks.

Girl, seeing:
experiencing challenges.

Glass breaking:
disaster, fright, panic, death of loved relatives.

Glass, bursting while holding it:
separation.

Glass, cutting:
something to investigate, to find out.

Glass, giving as a gift:
being well and fondly remembered.

Glass, seeing:
uncertainty in business, doubtful success.

Glide:
beware of allurement.

Globe, seeing or having:
going on a big trip, soon to be happily married.

Glory, well-deserved:
be careful of flatterers.

Gloves, having:
diminishing suspicion.

Gloves, seeing or putting on:
honour and happiness.

Glowing (fire), warming yourself:
quarrel with a friend.

Goat, billy goat, seeing jumping:
playing with tricks.

Goat, billy goat, being pushed by:
arguments ahead.

Goats, seeing:
comfort.

Goblet (cup), drinking from:
lots of fun at dinner party.

God, hearing him talk:
joyfulness.

God, praying to him:
joy.

God, praising:
means suffering.

God, seeing or talking to him:
worries and grief.

God, worshipping or attending mass:
peace of mind and calmness.

God, worshipping, yourself celebrating mass:
hard and depressing work ahead.

Going astray:
many difficulties.

Gold bars, receiving:
unpleasantness, annoyance.

Gold (coins), seeing or getting:
being truly loved, soon to be married.

Goldfinch (bird):
interesting acquaintance.

Goldfish:
obstacles in business ventures.

Gold, giving as a present:
attending a wedding.

Gold, losing:
being robbed, or cheated in business.

Gold mine, discovering:
a sure gain, definite profit.

Gold, playing with:
separation of friends, misfortune in ventures.

Gold, seeing or owning:
means flourishing success in started business.

Gold, stealing:
losing respect, or your lover.

Gold and silver dishes:
a flatterer is near you.

Gold, wearing:
fickleness, inconsistent.

Gooseberry, eating or seeing:
getting a grouchy husband or nagging wife.

Goose eggs:
    finding your good nutrition.

Goose meat, eating:
    lots of happiness.

Gorge (ravine), falling into:
    bad omen.

Gospel:
    receiving good advice and sympathy.

Gout pain:
    forthcoming danger, experiencing unpleasantness.

Grain (corn), nice ones:
    abundance, wealth.

Grain, cutting:
    joy.

Grain field, harvesting:
    big earnings.

Grain field, seeing:
    luck in love and ventures.

Grain, receiving:
    joy, profit, gain.

Grandchildren, your own:
    lasting, well-being.

Grandparents, seeing or talking:
    a good plan, executed.

Grapes, seeing:
    blue: bad luck; white: joy; red: affliction

Grapes, bunches, cutting:
    unexpected separation.

Grapes, getting as a present:
    acquaintance.

Grass, seeing:
    be alert about profiteers.

Grasshopper, seeing:
    happiness is of a short duration.

Grass (cutting):
good times, wealth.

Grater:
being pursued by evil people.

Grave, climbing in:
false friends, defame, pursuit.

Grave, climbing out of it:
being lucky in ventures, receiving gifts, late marriage.

Grave, closing up with soil:
regaining your health.

Grave, preparing:
losing a friend.

Grave, seeing being prepared:
death of a relative.

Grave, someone is being carried out:
helping a friend, a friend becomes your beneficiary.

Grave, seeing:
patience leads to goals.

Grave, with green grass:
hope and wishes coming true.

Gravedigger, seeing:
becoming sick.

Green peas, crunching and emptying them:
efforts in vain.

Greeted, being:
is bad.

Groom to be, or thinking you are:
disaster, loss of a friend or lover.

Grove, seeing:
going astray.

Grouse (white), flying:
unexpected news.

Guarantor, becoming:
for those ill, good; for those healthy, lots of expenses.

Guarantor, acceptance:
    big disadvantage.

Guard, seeing:
    be careful with whom you are acquainted.

Guests, accommodate:
    friendship being returned.

Guests, bid farewell:
    separation from a favoured thing.

Guests, welcoming:
    soon to have visitors.

Guests, strange once, shelter:
    unexpected happiness.

Guilty, being:
    ill once, death; healthy, bad omen.

Guinea fowl:
    saving, modesty, leads to a worry-free retirement.

Guitar, playing or hearing:
    happy party.

Guns, seeing:
    much repulsiveness.

Gun powder:
    being drawn to a dangerous gang

Hail, damage caused:
    disaster and illness.

Hailstorm, seeing:
    unpleasantness, annoyance, treason, wishes and hopes
    diminish.

Hair, braiding:
    connections come about.

Hair curls, seeing:
    becoming arrogant.

Hair combing:
    luck in all business activities, dissolving disagreements.

Hair, entangled:
family quarrel.

Hair, nice and black:
health.

Hair, grey having:
burdened with worries.

Hair, having red:
enemies.

Hair, not wearing your own:
forthcoming illness

Hair, seeing long:
being loved and respected.

Hair, makeup:
a jolly party lies ahead.

Hair, losing:
going through bad times.

Hair, shear off:
ease to worries.

Hair, to see it being sheared off:
getting out of adverse matters.

Hairdresser, seeing or talking to:
distress.

Hair, plaited, seeing:
the old things are not always the best.

Hall, bright, beautiful chandeliers and dancing in it:
great joy about a reconciliation.

Hall, beautifully furnished:
coming into your desired living standard.

Halberd, seeing:
bloody fight, bloodshed.

Ham, eating:
having many children, forthcoming wealth.

Ham, seeing:
reward and bonuses.

Hammer, seeing:
    brutal treatment, hard labour.

Hammer, using to work with:
    good progress in your work.

Hand, amputating:
    disaster ahead.

Handbasket, holding:
    worries about the future.

Handcuffed, being:
    cheat.

Handkerchief:
    cleanliness is good for your health.

Hands, swollen:
    unsociable, quarrelsome.

Hands, washing:
    to be honoured.

Hands, being wounded or dirty:
    disadvantage, despise.

Hang, seeing a person:
    to come to honour.

Hanging, to witness one:
    illness.

Hanging, seeing yourself:
    misfortune.

Hanging yourself, or being hanged:
    fear and misery ahead.

Harbour, seeing:
    delightful news, happiness and honour.

Harm, endure:
    being honoured.

Harness, wearing:
    rage leads to nastiness.

Harrow:
    losses and illness.

Harp, seeing or playing:
disappointment.

Harpist:
be careful about reckless company.

Harvest, good and being present:
wishes soon to be coming true.

Harvest, bringing home:
inheritance.

Harvesting in bad weather:
bad omen.

Hat, wearing, nice looking:
advantage, luck and recognition.

Hawk, seeing:
jealousy.

Hay, bad smelling, rotten:
disruption in business.

Haywagon:
effort brings progress.

Hazelnuts, cracking:
obtaining good profit.

Head, another person's cut off:
good ventures ahead.

Head, amputated:
falseness and fraud from people around you.

Head band:
occupying yourself with vanity, makeup and attire is defacing you.

Head, bald, seeing:
slander.

Head, extremely large, carrying:
triumph over your enemies, honour and dignity ahead.

Head of a black-skinned person, seeing:
good news from distant friends or relatives.

Head, shaving:
> dangerous, serious illness.

Head, washing:
> avoiding a disaster.

Head, without body, seeing:
> happiness and blessings.

Head with tangled hair:
> twist, quarrel.

Hearing loss:
> carelessness.

Heart, bleeding:
> offence, insult.

Heart, cutting up:
> separation of a loving couple.

Heart, eating:
> finding out being assertive, love is being returned.

Heart, seeing:
> tender loving.

Hedgehog, seeing:
> your goodness is being used.

Heel, injured:
> bad luck of all kinds.

Hell, as described, seeing or being in it:
> indicates changes of all kinds, suggested carefulness in ventures.

Hell, being rescued from:
> peace, courtesies, support.

Hemp, tied together:
> union is near.

Hemp, spin:
> household activities.

Hen, big and nice, seeing:
> happiness in loving.

Hen, hearing one cluck:
> good and prosperous wedding, marriage.

Hen ladder, seeing:
effort leads to prosperity.

Hen, squealing:
disaster, annoyance.

Hen, seeing:
forthcoming insult, offence.

Hen, with chicks, seeing:
lots of children, grandchildren, overall, large family.

Herbs, eating:
long life.

Herbs, searching for:
mischief, gain.

Herd, seeing on prairie or meadows:
prosperous future.

Herring, eating:
avoid drinking parties.

Hermit, seeing:
grief, worries.

Hip, having a big one:
being blessed with descendants.

Hitting someone:
you have to defend yourself.

Hole in cloth:
carelessness.

Hole, crawling in:
coming into hostile company.

Home, apartment:
changes ahead.

Honey, eating:
discomfort, misery.

Hood:
get together, with a big fool.

Hop:
your ventures will prosper.

Horn (bell), turning:
>getting out of sticky situation.

Hornet:
>news brings a lot of unrest and confusion.

Horns, having yourself:
>to be fooled.

Horns, from livestock, seeing:
>is not good at all.

Horseback rider, being thrown:
>experiencing humiliation in your pride.

Horseback rider:
>honour and dignity.

Horseback rider dismounting:
>losing a friend.

Horseback rider, mount:
>prosperity.

Horse, seeing bolt:
>coming into danger of death through carelessness.

Horse, tumbling, falling:
>bad luck lies ahead.

Horse harness:
>pleasant, worry-free life.

Horses, seeing or owning:
>happiness and lots of joy.

Horses, seeing in front of a carriage:
>soon to expect noble visitors.

Horses, thin, seeing:
>losing your good reputation.

Horse stable:
>effort and patience leading towards your goals.

Horse tail:
>distinction, dignity.

Horse shoe, seeing:
>soon to go on a trip.

Horse shoe, to see it being put on:
efforts and hard work.

Horse, being stubbed:
losing your lover.

Hospital:
coming into disgrace and shame.

House, being built:
luck in business and love, good and loyal servants.

House, being in it, and leaving:
gain, profit, advantage.

House, being demolished:
getting rid of an obstacle.

House, climbing towards:
happiness, triumph, victory.

House, falling from deep down:
careful in all deeds.

Household items, seeing a lot:
happiness in your marriage.

House, in ruins or collapsing:
disaster, unexpected case of death, losing your lover.

House, old, seeing:
long time friends, seeing again.

Hound:
bad business deals.

Hourglass, seeing:
a reminder that your lifespan on earth is limited.

Howling, hearing:
slander.

Hyacinth:
receiving a gift.

Hymn, singing or hearing:
a soon to be festivity.

Human feces:
(see People's feces)

Hungry:
> prosperity and honour are a result of diligence and saving.

Hunt:
> be patient, a happy future lies ahead.

Hunter:
> a lot of effortless work.

Hunting, deer:
> plans and projects are ruined.

Hunting, huge gems:
> means great success in ventures.

Hurricane, violent:
> losing your fortune.

Hut (cabin), seeing or being in it:
> hard work.

J

Ice, seeing or gliding on:
> near accident, pursuit, cheated in love, scattered hopes.

Ice, seeing in summer:
> useless start.

Icicles, hanging from your roof:
> your love for each other grows deeper.

Island, seeing or being there:
> abandoned by friends.

Illumination, seeing:
> funny, joyful days ahead.

Imperfection, experiencing:
> effort and work in vain.

Imprisonment:
> comforting friends.

Infantry:
> price hikes, bad times.

Infirmary, military hospital, being present at:
> long-lasting illness.

Inheritance, receiving:
>   misery and grief.

Ink, seeing:
>   reconciliation with your enemy.

Ink, spilling:
>   discord.

Ink pot, overturning:
>   hostility and repulsiveness.

Ink, writing with:
>   starting a new business.

Insane people, seeing:
>   anger and revenge.

Inscription on graves, reading:
>   loss of a family member.

Insects, seeing:
>   losses, gossip, illness.

Instruments, musical, seeing:
>   misadventure, death of a relative or acquaintance.

Intestines, seeing:
>   joy and love.

Insulted, being ill-treated:
>   annoyance and disagreement with household members.

Intoxicated:
>   property, fortune, growth.

Invalid:
>   caution, illness.

Itching (skin):
>   you are going to make a mistake.

Iron:
>   a lot of troublesome work.

Ivory:
>   poverty.

J

Jaundice:
great wealth, unexpected good fortune.

Jewish person, seeing or dealing with:
betrayal, deception.

Jewish person, receiving service from:
unexpected luck, advantage in all matters.

Jewelry, seeing or wearing:
a nice gift awaits you.

Joy (feeling):
be careful, foolishness.

Joyful in your sleep:
unrest.

Jubilate:
disaster and sadness.

Judge, seeing or talking to:
boring business.

Judgement:
unpleasant news.

Judging, execution witnessing:
false love, unfaithfulness.

Jug (pitcher):
luck, joy, avoiding danger.

Juggler, seeing:
beware of fraud.

Juice, handing to a sick person:
privileges.

Juice, squeezing:
worry about the future.

Jumping into water:
danger, losing a friend or an acquaintance.

Jumping over a ditch, creek or fence:
overcoming imminent danger, avoiding a hostile plot.

Juniper:
bad gossip.

K

Kabal, playing:
contempt.

Kettle:
you are well-accepted.

Kettle (drum):
big worries ahead.

Key, finding:
getting around embarrassment.

Key, losing:
ambiance, dispute.

Key, using:
suspicion.

Keychain:
managing a household gives lots of joy.

Killed, being yourself:
fear and hardship.

King or queen, seeing or talking to:
forthcoming honour, good business deals, achieving wealth.

Kissing a married person:
bad omen of misfortune and disagreements.

Kissing a man, or seeing a man kissing:
being unexpectedly deserted by friends.

Kissing nice girls:
true and good friends.

Kissing somebody's hand:
happiness and cheerfulness.

Kissing, wanting to:
　grief and depression.

Kitchen, cooking:
　gossip.

Kitchen, seeing:
　defamation

Knee, damaged seeing:
　poverty, declining business.

Knee, laying on it:
　humiliation.

Knee, swollen:
　illness, effort, losses.

Knife, with a nice handle:
　receiving gifts, very soon.

Knife, seeing or holding:
　persecution, disgrace, poverty, failing business.

Knight:
　winning over a truthful friend.

Knitting:
　diligence and perseverance make your plans succeed.

Knitted things, seeing:
　bad omen, being fooled.

Knot, seeing:
　embarrassment.

Knot, making:
　causing others embarrassment.

Knot, undoing:
　confusion, clearing up.

Labyrinth, seeing:
　removal of all obstacles.

Labyrinth, walking through:
　discovering secrets.

Laboratory:
>serious illness.

Lackey (footman):
>unexpected great joy.

Ladder, seeing or using:
>improvement of situation, wealth and honour, happy marriage.

Ladder, placing:
>being robbed.

Lady's maid:
>laziness is dangerous.

Laying out, offering:
>good, for the poor.

Lamb, seeing hopping:
>enjoying children.

Lamp:
>giving out information.

Lamp, turning off:
>destroying another's good prospects.

Lance, seeing or carrying:
>disagreements, efforts in vain.

Landscape, scenery:
>pleasant, fun trip.

Land, bare and deserted, seeing:
>misfortune, annoyance, depression.

Land, beautiful, seeing:
>getting a good wife.

Land, big and wide, seeing:
>joy, amusement, fun, riches.

Land, strange and unknown:
>loss of money, bad luck.

Land, prepared with lots of fruit, seeing:
>good harvest, succeeding in ventures.

Lantern, burning:
>exposing secrets.

Lap, sitting on:
>fondness.

Lard, seeing:
>forthcoming difficulties.

Lark (bird), seeing:
>rapid rise, success

Larkspur (flower):
>being rescued from danger.

Last will (testament), drafting:
>misfortune and dissatisfaction.

Last will (testatment), seeing someone else's:
>advantage and unexpected joy.

Lattice fence, facing:
>freeing yourself, inner peace.

Laugh, hearing:
>experiencing sudden joy.

Lavatory (toilet):
>annoyance, boredom.

Law (claim), defending:
>receiving recognition.

Lawyers, dealing with:
>sorrow.

Lawsuit:
>loyal friends.

Lawn, seeing or sitting on:
>adventurous life.

Lead, being burned by:
>falling into temptation.

Lead bullets, loading:
>bad conscience.

Lead, melting:
>hard days ahead.

Lead, seeing:
> wrongful prosecution.

Leaves, dry, withered:
> interference in your plans.

Leaves, falling:
> becoming dangerously ill.

Leaves, green, seeing:
> experiencing pleasantness.

Learning (studying):
> effort and endurance are overcoming all difficulties.

Leather:
> complicated business ventures.

Leech, seeing:
> self-interest.

Lecture, giving or hearing:
> your efforts are being rewarded.

Leg, artificial:
> enduring bad changes.

Leg, having a swollen or ill one:
> betrayal by friends, loss of a beloved one.

Leg, seeing being amputated:
> losing a good friend.

Leg, seeing hurt:
> misfortune.

Leg, strong, or seeing your own:
> happiness, joy and success.

Lemon, eating or seeing:
> happiness and peace of mind.

Lemon, squeezing:
> being abused.

Lemonade, drinking:
> invitation to a dinner party.

Lentil, eating:
> annoyance and separation.

Lentil, dispersing:
>harming yourself.

Lentil, seeing:
>quarrel.

Lepers, keeping company with:
>experiencing unpleasantness.

Lepers, seeing:
>worries and struggle.

Leprosy, having:
>promised great wealth, success in business.

Letter, receiving:
>means forthcoming wealth.

Letter-case, seeing or finding:
>resolving hidden matters.

Letters, burning:
>irresponsible blows, tricks.

Letters, important, receiving:
>means continuation in a good way, whatever you have started.

Letters, opening those addressed to others:
>annoyance.

Letters, reading:
>trust enjoying.

Letters, sealing:
>keeping secrets.

Letters, seeing, to be read:
>request = be careful.

Letters, tearing, or torn, seeing:
>ugly slander, giving up a good friend.

Letters, writing:
>not the slightest chance, untrustworthiness.

Lettuce, eating:
>good prospect.

Lettuce, sowing:
>starting useless things.

Library, seeing or own:
finding good advice.

Lice, seeing or having:
receiving money.

Lice, killing:
avoiding an ugly persecution.

Life, losing your own:
unsuccessful business.

Light, bright, burning:
health and prosperity, a soon engagement.

Light, carrying, blown out by wind:
sudden death.

Light, faded, seeing:
happy trip ahead.

Light of any kind, seeing extinguished:
forthcoming bad luck, losing a fight, disagreement.

Light or torch, extinguished, seeing:
sadness, sickness, poverty.

Lightening, seeing:
argument, disagreement, annoyance.

Lilies, seeing:
power and wealth.

Lilac tree:
illness and worries

Limb, losing a section of:
relief from something bad.

Limbs, deformed, seeing:
scare ahead.

Limp:
your good reputation is in jeopardy.

Limp, seeing someone else:
ignorance endured.

Linden tree:
fulfillment of your wishes.

Linen, fine quality:
enjoying happy days.

Linen, trading:
prosperous business.

Linnet, bird, seeing or hearing:
joy and good news from faraway relatives or friends.

Lion, seeing:
gaining wealth, respect from your superior, marrying a well-educated, rich lady.

Lion, locked up:
fear and difficulty.

Lion, killing:
overcoming your enemy.

Lions pursuing you:
being deserted.

Lion with cubs, seeing:
coming into danger.

Lips, beautiful, red, having or seeing:
prosperity and health of distant friends or relatives.

Liquor:
avoid flatterers.

Little, being:
a rise in your status.

Liver, eating:
steady health.

Liver, cutting apart:
destroying your own health.

Liver, seeing:
having good, nutritious food.

Livery:
for servants, good; for masters, disadvantage

Livestock (herd), seeing:
prosperity.

Livestock, put to pasture:
disgrace, annoyance.

Lizard, seeing:
  big chances in business.

Load, carrying:
  fast, finishing business matters.

Loam (pit):
  you are being followed.

Locksmith:
  getting to know a secret.

Locked up:
  loss of happiness.

Logging (wood):
  a death.

Locomotive:
  beware daydreamer (your head is in the clouds).

Lost, your belongings:
  judge your own opinion, and you will be well off.

Lottery draw:
  big losses.

Lotto, playing:
  cozy company.

Lover, seeing or being alone together:
  temptation.

Luck, having or sudden wealth:
  pursued by friends, harassed by creditors.

Lunar eclipse:
  losing your girlfriend.

Lute, playing:
  pleasant company

Lye, drinking or seeing:
  repulsiveness.

Lynx, seeing:
  discovering a person's cleverness.

M

Magic:
  beware of swindlers.

Magnet, seeing or having:
  being liked.

Magpie, seeing:
  cheat.

Maid, girl, seeing:
  happiness, and soon being united.

Makeup, using:
  treason, falseness.

Malformation, deformity, seeing:
  being hurt through slander.

Male nurse:
  you are earning love and gratefulness.

Man, with nightcap:
  too much comfort is not good for you.

Man (noble), elegant, seeing:
  obnoxious people.

Manure, seeing:
  dishonoured through bad company.

Manure, loading:
  servitude for a long time.

Manure wagon, driving:
  unpleasant work.

Maps, seeing:
  a trip lies ahead.

Marble, seeing:
  getting in and out of arguments.

Marketplace, seeing:
  difficulty and hardship.

Marmot, seeing:
  poverty and laziness.

Marten, killing:
freeing yourself of unpleasantness.

Marten, shooting:
good business with strangers.

Marriage (settling down):
sadness.

Marrow, dumpling, preparing:
making a good living.

Marrow, finding in legs:
great wealth and happiness.

Masquerade, seeing:
being cheated.

Mass, attending:
inner peace.

Mass, celebrating by yourself:
getting difficult and depressing work.

Masquerade, making:
prosperous business.

Mask (face), seeing or wearing:
warning, hypocritical friends.

Matches, using or seeing:
riches, treasures.

Mats, straw, watching being made:
food shortage.

Mattress, seeing:
restlessness.

Mattress, laying on it:
pleasant relations.

Matron, seeing:
reaching an old age.

Meadow:
on a pleasant excursion.

Meal, having:
stinginess and poverty.

Meal, having with company:
abundance and riches.

Measles:
many hours of enjoyment.

Meat, feeding the dogs:
scornful treatment.

Meat, prepared, eating:
prosperity.

Meat, raw, bought by others:
arguments, disagreement.

Meat, raw, seeing or buying:
supportive friends, forthcoming wealth and honour.

Medal, seeing:
neglect.

Medal (decoration), seeing or receiving:
coming into honour and reputation.

Medaler, eating or seeing:
getting a good husband and having beautiful children.

Medicine, bitter taste:
repression from your enemies.

Medicine, to see being prescribed:
continuation of illness.

Medicine, handing others:
advantage and benefit.

Medicine, discharge through intestines:
good business deals.

Medicine (roots), seeing or eating:
end of annoying business.

Medicine, seeing:
indisposition.

Medicine, spitting out:
bad luck, trouble in your business transaction.

Medicine, taking:
repulsiveness.

Medicine, using:
 loss of money.

Meeting a friend:
 good.

Meeting an enemy:
 bad.

Mellows, seeing or eating:
 unshakable love in marriage, an unsatisfying entertainer.

Merry-go-round, riding on or seeing:
 coming into entanglements.

Merchandise, buying or selling:
 activity in business brings huge profit.

Mercury:
 unsteady, restless life.

Mermaid:
 treason or prosecution.

Meteorological observation:
 pursued by false friends.

Mice, seeing or catching:
 successful business, good marriage and prosperity.

Mice, squeaking:
 falling into grief.

Microscope, looking through:
 try to improve your flaws.

Midwife, seeing or talking to:
 happiness, publication of a secret.

Milk, drinking or eating:
 advancing in your occupation, through economics.

Milk, buying:
 success in a lot of things.

Milk truck:
 going on a nice trip.

Mill, seeing in operation:
 happiness and riches.

Mill stone, seeing:
> growing family.

Mill wheel, getting caught in:
> coming into great danger.

Millet, eating:
> family life, big estate.

Milt:
> festivities, fun.

Mine, seeing:
> growth of wealth and property.

Miner, seeing:
> unwanted visitor.

Mirror, breaking:
> hostility.

Mirror, seeing:
> for healthy people, joy and honour; for ill people, death.

Mirror, seeing yourself in:
> being betrayed.

Mirror, with golden frame:
> better status through extraordinary circumstances.

Miserable feeling:
> worrisome days.

Misery, great, seeing:
> contempt.

Mist (fog), covering the sun:
> eye illness.

Mist (fog), disappearing:
> being cleared of false accusations.

Mist (fog), dense:
> encountering complex matters

Mite, maggot, seeing:
> dispute at home.

Molasses:
> using tricks to get you.

Mole, seeing:
injury, harm.

Monastery, seeing:
rest and peaceful old age.

Money, copper:
effortless work.

Money, counting:
happiness, great fortune.

Money exchange, stock trading:
lots of luck.

Money, finding:
profit, gain, good prospect for the future.

Money, full bags of:
secure, pleasant future.

Money, losing:
embarrassment, bad circumstances.

Money, metal, finding:
becoming happy.

Money, metal, paying with:
increasing respect.

Money, metal, receiving:
getting along well, joy.

Money, metal, seeing:
joyfulness, profit.

Money, paying with it:
freeing yourself from a burden.

Money, receiving:
nervousness, unrest.

Money, seeing:
falling into temptation.

Money, wallet, full:
good progress in ventures.

Money, wallet, empty:
sustaining losses.

Monk, seeing:
being in good company.

Monks, talking to:
reconciliation, coming to terms with your offenders.

Monkey, long-tailed:
illness, disgust.

Monster, seeing:
much misfortune, annoyance, false hopes.

Monument, seeing:
sickness.

Moon, bright shining:
sincere joy, being truly loved.

Moon, seeing its first quarter:
succeeding in love and trade.

Moon, seeing through the water (reflection):
pleasant acquaintance.

Moon, seeing decline:
fading love, damage in trade.

Moor (land), dry, seeing:
prevention of any hope.

Moor (land), green, seeing:
the last beam of hope.

Morgue, visiting or seeing:
deadly peril, losing a friend.

Mortar:
great festivity, pleasant visitors.

Moss:
coming into much money.

Mosquito:
bad company will bring you down.

Mother, seeing or talking to:
seeing a disappointed friend again.

Mountain, climbing:
effort, unpleasantness.

Mountain, climbing, not reaching the top:
   declining ventures.

Mountain, collapsing:
   being trailed by a powerful enemy.

Mountain, descending:
   small but solid profit.

Mountains, seeing with green trees:
   hope for the future.

Mountains, seeing with beautiful castles:
   steadfast, firmness.

Mountains with ruins:
   interruption in your plans.

Mouse trap:
   beware of persecution.

Mouth, can't open:
   deadly peril.

Mouth, huge:
   mark of respect, enjoying esteem.

Mouth organ, playing or seeing:
   good news.

Mower, seeing at work:
   luck and blessings in business.

Mower, seeing resting:
   losing friends.

Moveable goods, selling:
   getting involved in lawsuits.

Muddy, dirty cloth, wearing:
   misfortune and grief.

Mud, sludge, walking through:
   difficult times ahead.

Muffs, wearing or seeing:
   terrible times are coming.

Mule, seeing or riding:
   being deceived and fooled by others.

Mulberry tree:
wealth and blessed years ahead.

Mulberries, eating or seeing:
late but happy marriage.

Murder, you being:
fright, shock experiencing.

Mushrooms:
falseness brings great drawbacks.

Mushrooms, eating or seeing:
reaching an old age.

Music, beautiful:
receiving good, merry news.

Mussels, seeing:
bad news from far away, embarrassment that takes great effort to eliminate.

Mustache:
idle, transient joy.

Mustard, coarse, eating or seeing:
bad omen.

Mustard, fine, seeing:
suffering from gossip.

Myrtle tree:
happily in love, enjoying respect, marrying a nice girl.

Myrtle, crown:
soon to be married.

Nails, finding:
luck, happiness.

Naked, yourself being:
ridicule and lots of sufferings.

Naked, seeing others:
luck and bright days ahead.

Navel, seeing:
increasing your wealth.

Neck, big and thick:
> happiness.

Neck, small and thin:
> misfortune.

Neck (throat), being choked by a person:
> that same person will influence you.

Neck (throat), seeing:
> good omen.

Neck (throat), swollen:
> happiness.

Necklace, neck ribbon, seeing:
> honour and happiness.

Necklace, wearing:
> to be privileged, honoured.

Necktie, seeing:
> for the not-so-fortunate, a good omen; for the fortunate, losses or imprisonment.

Necktie, taking off:
> being protected against a cold.

Need, being in need:
> forthcoming bad luck.

Needles, seeing or using:
> arguments.

Negro, seeing:
> disaster in undertakings.

Neighbour, seeing or talking to:
> coming into danger.

Nets:
> corruption will bring harm.

Nettle:
> libel, pursuit.

Nest, empty, seeing:
> happy marriage.

Nest, full, seeing:
> additions to the family.

Night birds, seeing:
    never start anything before thinking it over twice.

Nightingale, seeing or hearing sing:
    joyful news in your engagement time, happy marriage.

Night owl, flying:
    chaos between your loved ones.

Night owl, on top of house, and crying:
    a bad omen.

Night watchman:
    thieves, causing harm.

Nose, big, your own:
    obtaining wealth and honour.

Nose, bleeding:
    enduring ignorance.

Nose, short:
    modest circumstances, but happy, peaceful family life.

Nose, clogged:
    an influential man is leaving you, defraud trust and friendship.

Noise, turmoil:
    nervousness and restlessness in the house.

Northern lights, seeing:
    your nicest dreams and hopes come true.

Notary, consulting:
    soon to be married.

Notary, seeing him/her write:
    being mentioned in an inheritance.

Numbers, seeing:
    through stupidity, you will lose a lot.

Numbers, picking those you favour in a draw:
    good prospect of big earnings.

Numbers, writing:
    getting lots to do.

Numbers, seeing:
    under 90, uncertainty; over 90, luck and prosperity

Numbers, seeing and not remembering:
merry, fun social gathering.

Numbness, freeze:
work in vain.

Nun, seeing or talking to:
entering a different social status.

Nuts, eating or seeing:
wealth, happiness and honour.

Nuts, playing with:
arguments.

Nuts, walnuts, seeing:
annoyance and misfortune.

Oak tree, beautiful, seeing:
advantage, wealth, long life.

Oak tree, dried out:
death of a relative or friend.

Oath, to take or see being taken:
involvement in lawsuits.

Obelisk, seeing:
surprised through extraordinary events.

Ocean, or big sea, crossing:
disaster.

Ocean:
(see, "sea")

Ocean birds, seeing:
for travelers on sea, danger.

Offence, being offended:
favour and kindness.

Office, being there:
great losses, your debtor lets you down.

Oil, beating with mixer:
competition, appeal.

Oil, burning:
much effort in vain.

Oil, being poured over you:
advantage.

Oil, good tasting:
strong health.

Oil, seeing spilled:
tremendous losses.

Oil, saving, scratching up:
luck and advantage.

Ointment, making:
illness.

Old, being:
liberty, freedom.

Old, becoming:
evil, bad.

Olives:
fond of sweetness, hasty behaviour.

Onions, cooking:
coming into needs, being bothered by authorities.

Onion, eating:
grief.

Onions, seeing:
secrets are being revealed.

Opera glass:
news awaiting.

Opponent, meeting with him:
misfortune.

Oranges, eating or seeing:
suffering from lingering indisposition.

Oranges, bitter tasting:
loss of honour and wealth, being misjudged.

Orchard, walking through:
becoming rich because of inheritance, happy marriage, many good children, true love, influential friends.

Organ, seeing or hearing being played:
joy or inheritance.

Ornament (jewelry), seeing:
vanity creates heartbreak.

Ostrich:
making a fuss about nothing.

Otter, fish, catching:
luck in business.

Overcoat:
seeing great dignitaries.

Owls, crying:
vexation, annoyance.

Owls, seeing:
discontentedness, illness, poverty.

Ox, seeing at work:
servitude, bondage.

Ox, seeing:
advantage in trade affairs.

Ox, to see jumping:
coming into danger.

Oysters, eating or seeing:
success in your work, happy pregnancy.

Pail or water bucket, seeing:
comfort.

Pain, feeling:
hardship, luckily overcoming trouble.

Painting, seeing a portrait of yourself:
long life.

Painting something white:
pursuit, persecution.

Painting something black:
illness.

Painting something rotten:
joy.

Painting, seeing:
being tempted by false friends, danger, deceived by lover,
loss of a friend

Palace:
arrogance brings you down.

Palisade, conquering or destroying:
security, glory, happiness.

Palisade, seeing:
embarrassment and restlessness.

Palm, branches, seeing, carrying or collecting:
abundance, wealth, luck in business.

Panther, seeing:
being frightened.

Pantry, seeing:
sickness and bad luck.

Paper, cutting:
worries about the future.

Paper, printed, seeing:
trustworthy.

Paper, tearing apart:
coming into anger.

Paper, writing on:
suing and defamation.

Parade, seeing:
the thirst for pleasure brings big disadvantage.

Paradise, being in it:
being identified with a lovely thing.

Paralyzed:
misery, hardship.

Parcel, carrier:
effort and work keeps a healthy spirit.

Parchment:
unexpected inheritance brings joy.

Parents, arguing with them:
bad omen.

Parents, seeing or talking to:
good fortune in ventures, cheerfulness.

Parents, siblings, seeing deceased:
confusion, bad luck.

Park, seeing:
a comfortable life.

Parrot, seeing:
coming to know of secrets.

Parrot, talking:
disgusting gossip.

Party, attending a social gathering:
danger of one's life.

Partridge, seeing:
mad desires.

Pass (mountain):
hard, troublesome work.

Passport:
going on a big trip.

Pasture (land), seeing:
danger and difficulty.

Path, walking on a wide one:
happiness.

Path, walking on a small one:
grief and annoyance.

Pavement, seeing:
bad omen in every way.

Pawn shop:
recklessness leads to losses.

Pawn shop, entering:
bad business.

Peaches, breaking in half:
coming into your desired lifestyle.

Peaches, seeing or eating:
reunion with your estranged lover.

Peacock, seeing:
rapid progress in ventures, many lucky connections, many courtesies on a trip.

Pearl, seeing or owning:
misfortune, discomfort.

Pearls, sorting:
lonely, boring life.

Pear tree, shaking:
intemperate.

Pears, beautiful looking, hanging on a tree:
good prospect for the future.

Pears, being eaten by insects:
insidiousness.

Pears, good ones, seeing or eating:
overcoming disagreements.

Pears, sour, eating or seeing:
annoyance in your household.

Peas, eating:
luck in ventures.

Peas, planting:
hopes in succeeding of your plans.

Peas, seeing or picking:
prosperity, growing wealth, cheerfulness.

Peas, nice, growing and blooming:
good progress in your deeds.

Pencils:
receiving a good message.

Penitentiary:
rescue from imminent danger.

Pennant, seeing:
>people of authority favour you.

Penny:
>charity brings reward.

People, coming towards you:
>sadness, affliction.

People, dressed in black:
>coming into danger of death.

People, seeing many:
>bad luck, disaster.

People's feces (stool), seeing:
>great wealth.

People's feces (stool), stepping into:
>getting an unexpected large fortune.

People, old, seeing:
>good luck.

People, old, honouring:
>lots of blessings.

Pepper, seeing or using:
>being offended.

Pursuing:
>unpleasantness.

Petrol:
>risky wanderings.

Petticoat, colourful, seeing:
>doubtful success in love or otherwise business.

Petticoat, white, seeing:
>a rare enjoyment.

Pharmacy, seeing, being in it:
>meeting with profiteers and evil people.

Piano, playing or seeing:
>dispute, conflict between friends.

Pictures, beautiful, seeing:
>being cheated.

Pictures, seeing big and bad looking ones:
finding friends, getting happy.

Pie's pastries:
excess leads to illness.

Pig's seeing:
deceived by servants, remove unpleasantness.

Pig, rolling in the mud:
getting a evil housekeeper.

Pig shed:
disadvantaged business.

Pike seeing:
coming into danger.

Pill:
beware of folly and fools.

Pilgrim seeing:
news from abroad.

Pilgrimage:
your start is commandable.

Pillar seeing:
honour.

Pillar collapsing:
invalidism, illness.

Pin-cushion (needles):
a nice gift will surprise you.

Pin, seeing or having:
getting lots of rewarding work.

Pineapple eating:
being invited as a guest.

Pipe:
pleasant circumstances.

Pistol:
pursuit by enemies.

Pit, seeing or falling into:
sudden misfortune, being tricked.

Pit, climbing out with great effort:
  pursuit, having unknown friends.

Pit, getting out easy:
  overcoming many big difficulties.

Pith (stone) collecting:
  a long lasting plan, becomes reality.

Pyramid's climbing:
  good business.

Pyramid's seeing:
  happiness and honour.

Place, seeing:
  friendly reception.

Plains, seeing:
  happiness and enjoyment.

Planting:
  prosperity and authority prestige.

Plaster-ornaments:
  disaster about your plans.

Plaster (white wash):
  huge expenses are ahead.

Pliers, seeing:
  treason or pursuit.

Plow, your own or seeing one:
  soon to be happily married.

Plow, destroying:
  interruption in your trade, job.

Plowing:
  good progress in business.

Plums, eating or seeing:
  bad times ahead.

Plums (Italian), oval, freestone, eating:
  shock, sickness.

Plums (Italian), freestone, on trees:
  prosperous future.

Poison, giving somebody:
disagreement, annoyance.

Poison, taking and dying:
giving bad advice.

Pole, cat:
miserable illness.

Poles, stick:
disagreements.

Police:
repulsiveness, disagreements, ahead.

Pomegranates, seeing:
coming to wealth through a last will or luck.

Pond, seeing a little one:
getting a beautiful woman, wishes come true, joy from your family.

Pope, seeing or talking to:
happiness, cheerfulness.

Poplar, whisper or seeing:
good outcome of a project.

Poppy seed head, seeing:
becoming ill.

Porcupine:
warning about mockery and envy.

Pork meat:
remain in an ordinary social class.

Portraying yourself:
long life.

Portraying, by a painter:
having good friends.

Portrait, seeing:
long life for the person you have seen.

Portrait, your own, giving away:
treason, betrayal and disagreements.

Portrait, a beautiful girl:
soon to be married.

Portrait, carrying and breaking:
imminent disaster.

Portrait, seeing it being painted:
abide in your love.

Portrait, receiving as a gift:
lots of fun.

Post (stake), pushing into the ground:
effortless work.

Post wagon:
pleasant news.

Potatoes, digging:
effort, getting little thanks for hard work.

Potatoes, eating or seeing:
becoming ill.

Pots, seeing:
gaining wealth.

Pots, breaking:
fun party.

Poultry, feeding:
soon to be engaged.

Praying:
joy and peace of mind.

Prayer book:
comfort in sorrow.

Preaching:
moderate lifestyle keeps your health and well being.

Pregnant woman:
unpleasantness lies ahead.

Pregnant woman, making fun of:
being freed of worries.

Priest, standing in pulpit:
experiencing repulsiveness.

Prison, being released:
illness, death.

Prison building, seeing:
inner peace.

Prison, being escorted into:
happiness and well-being.

Procession, attending or seeing:
happiness and joy.

Profit, receiving:
arrival of a friend.

Profiteer, talking or doing business with:
illegal business temptation.

Profiteering:
shame, loss of fortune.

Property, estate, beautiful and large inheritance, receiving as a gift:
happy and profitable marriage.

Prostitute, seeing or talking to:
happy days and luck.

Prostration:
in company with dishonest friends.

Protection, finding:
misery, ramification.

Protractor:
you will start building.

Provoke:
hostility, discord.

Pub (inn) lodging:
staying calm during disagreements and complaints.

Pub (saloon), seeing:
getting rest.

Public festival, attending:
unstable luck, personal mishap.

Puddle:
corrupt company gives you a bad reputation.

Pulpit, standing in it, or seeing:
being honoured in public.

Pump in action:
surprises, very good omen.

Pump (well), empty or dry:
poverty, misfortune, bad luck.

Pumpkin, eating:
sickness.

Pumpkin, playing with:
separation from a favoured thing.

Pumpkins, seeing hanging:
having many mentors.

Puppet show, seeing:
getting a subordinate job.

Puppet:
loyal, devoted servants.

Purchasing, something:
extravagance, waste, brings disadvantage.

Purgatory:
be careful not to sin.

Purse bag, finding empty:
ungrateful.

Purse, finding with money:
no gain or profit.

Q

Quail, seeing or hearing:
dispute, treason, disagreement, unlucky in marriage.

Quarrel:
unexpected news.

Quackery:
stupidity brings harm.

Quince, seeing:
hapiness in marriage, wealth, peace of mind.

R

Rabbi:
soon to be in pleasant company.

Rabbit meat, eating:
peace of mind.

Rabbit, seeing:
fear, fearing death.

Rabbit, shooting:
being happy.

Radish:
simple nutrition keeps you healthy.

Rage, getting into:
a long overdue business matter comes to an end.

Rain, downpour, seeing:
efforts in vain.

Rain, downpour, coming into:
losing courage and balance.

Rain, seeing or being in it:
happiness in the family, constant love.

Rain, thunder and lightening, getting wet:
trouble ahead and bad luck.

Rainbow, seeing:
>lots of efforts in vain, troublesome luck.

Raisins:
>excessiveness brings ruin.

Rake:
>expect news.

Ram, being kicked or pushed by:
>pursuit.

Ram, seeing:
>profit.

Ranger, meeting:
>imminent mischief, unpleasantness.

Raped, being:
>disaster in any way.

Raped, in public:
>disaster and declining enterprises or ventures.

Rasp:
>a lot of uproar for nothing.

Raspberries, eating or seeing:
>enjoyment and pleasure are awaiting you.

Rats, catching:
>settling a dispute.

Rats, seeing:
>many enemies, decieved by friends.

Ravens claws, seeing:
>disaster and disagreements.

Raven, flying around you:
>death.

Reading:
>you will get good news.

Reaper:
>luck in business.

Receipt:
>losses ahead.

Reed, seeing in water:
  indecision brings drawbacks and disadvantage.

Relatives, seeing or talking:
  delusion, fraud.

Relic, seeing:
  danger of losing money and estate.

Resting:
  danger ahead.

Respect, showing:
  humiliation.

Respect, receiving:
  favourable establishments.

Restaurant, inn:
  great unrest ahead.

Restaurant, serving meals:
  creating hatred and envy.

Resurrection of the dead:
  rescue from misery.

Retailing:
  treason, pursuit.

Revenge:
  long-lasting involvement in lawsuit.

Review of troops:
  imprisonment.

Rib, seeing:
  happiness in the family, luck in business.

Rice, eating or seeing:
  plenty of money and assets are forthcoming.

Rich, being:
  in danger of losing everything.

Rich (wealthy) people, seeing, talking to or being friends with:
  receiving good deeds, comfort, reward.

Rifle, going hunting:
  unfaithfulness.

Rifle, seeing a nice looking one:
  falling in love.

Rifle, shooting one:
  big embarrassment.

Ring, hammering around a barrel:
  new connections.

Ring of gold and precious stones:
  coming into well-off circumstances.

Ring, finding:
  happiness lies ahead.

Ring, giving as a present:
  becoming a bride or groom.

Ring, losing:
  unexpected separation from a lover, friends or relatives.

Rivalry:
  unsuccessful ventures.

River, crossing over:
  overcome dangerous enemies.

River, crashing over rocks:
  a family member faces ruin.

River, falling into:
  misfortune.

River, overflowing:
  stop, project hindered.

River, being swept downstream:
  annoyance, danger, persecution.

River, roar:
  slander, blasphemy.

Roaring, howling of animals:
  bad news.

Roast beef, eating or seeing:
  profitable, good business.

Roast, smelling:
doing unnecessary errands.

Robber, being slayed by:
losing inheritance.

Robber, seeing or being held up by:
casual ties with relatives, children or fortunes.

Rock, ascending easily:
reaching your goals.

Rock, climbing:
conquest.

Rock, climbing and not reaching the top:
a stand still, decline in business.

Rock, descending from easily:
losing friends or relatives.

Rock, tall, seeing:
dealing with a huge project.

Rock, seeing:
work and effort.

Rocket, seeing rising:
changeable luck, unsteady in love, invitation to a happy party.

Rod, someone hitting:
advantage, overpowering.

Royalty, on horseback or in a carriage:
leaning towards wastefulness.

Royalty, seeing:
honour.

Royalty, talking to:
being envied.

Roof, full of swallows:
going on a trip.

Roof, eaves, standing under:
unpleasantness, difficulty.

Roof, falling down from:
unpleasant news.

Roof, seeing on a house:
domesticity, family life.

Room, sweeping:
effort and tenacity leads to your goal.

Rooms, nicely wallpapered:
flourishing trade.

Rope, being made:
means declining prosperity.

Rope, being tied up:
good fortune and honour.

Rope, cutting:
harming others.

Rope, climbing down it:
danger in your activities.

Rope dancer:
a risky venture brings harm.

Rooster, crowing:
caution.

Rooster, seeing:
being liked by women.

Roosters fighting:
difficulty in marriage.

Rosebuds:
discovery of a precious object.

Rosebush with many roses:
family additions.

Roses, seeing faded:
vexation, unsteady love, bad luck.

Roses, in full bloom:
happiness and blessings.

Rosemary, seeing:
coming into good reputation.

Rosehip, eating:
poverty.

Roots:
> secure living standard, being well-off.

Rowing:
> having hard, but rewarding work.

Ruins, seeing:
> being sloppy brings harm.

Rum, drinking:
> excessiveness damages health.

Running, and not moving ahead:
> much effort in vain.

Running, or seeing someone run:
> fulfillment of your wishes, being lucky.

Sabre:
> perseverance brings you towards your goal.

Sack, bag, heavy, carrying:
> harmful times.

Sacks, full, seeing:
> abundance in all earthly things.

Sack, being carried:
> lots of expenses.

Sack, seeing with holes:
> losses.

Sacks, many piled on a wagon:
> flourishing trade.

Sad, being:
> making friends.

Sad, being, not knowing why:
> very bad omen.

Sailor (seaman), seeing or talking to:
> misfortune on trips.

Sailor, arriving on a ship:
news from a friend or relative who lives far away.

Sailboat:
big trip ahead.

Saint, worship:
blessed at your work.

Salad:
a time of tests lies ahead.

Saliva and vomiting:
excess ruins your health.

Salmon, eating:
you will have a discovery.

Salt, scattering:
annoyance.

Sand, seeing:
insecurity in everything.

Sausage, eating:
unexpected visitor, flirtation.

Sausage, seeing or making:
struggle.

Saw, seeing your own:
a business deal is happily finalized.

Saw, seeing or using:
means good progress in your business.

Scabies (itch), having:
unnecessary fear and worries.

Scaffold, seeing:
be on guard.

Scandal:
disagreements, hostility.

Scare, being scared:
grief and food shortage.

Scarecrow:
having dishonest friends.

Scars, getting or having:
honour and glory.

Scepter:
demanding behaviour is disliked.

School, attending:
happiness.

School or school children, seeing:
being cheated, sorrow.

School teacher:
difficult and troublesome business.

Scissors:
involvement in something unpleasant.

Scissors, seeing:
gain, profit.

Scorpion, seeing:
be careful, malicious enemies.

Scuffle, fight:
don't get involved in the affairs of others.

Scythe, to own or see:
being offended by friends.

Scythe, mowing or seeing:
shows gain, profit, getting hard working servants.

Sea, calm, cruising:
happy union, coming into great riches.

Sea, cruising, landing on a deserted place:
with effort and difficulty you will reach your goal at last,
reward through success.

Sea, stormy, cruising:
lots of complaints in love or business.

Sea hog, seeing:
joyfulness.

Seal (signet ring) using:
coming out of threatening danger, enjoying security.

Sealing (letters):
many business deals.

Seats (chairs):
distinction.

Secluded (place), being there:
illness and danger.

Sedan, limousine, seeing:
pleasant future.

Seeds, picked by birds:
losing confidence.

Seed, selling:
flourishing business.

Seeds, sorting:
means good progress in business.

Seeing your deceased relatives and friends:
grief and sorrow.

Seminar, attending:
betrayal or being fooled.

Sentenced, seeing people:
losing some of your friends.

Sentry box, seeing:
being safe from enemies.

Seraglio:
exuberance is the ruin of soul and body.

Sewing kit:
increase in your income.

Sewing, stitching:
your work comes very handy.

Shadow, walking in it:
withdrawing from an oppressing relationship.

Sheaf, tying together:
new acquaintance.

Sheaf, loading, harvesting:
efforts are being rewarded.

Sheafs, seeing:
humiliation from your enemies.

Sheafs, lots of spikes, seeing:
good fortune.

Sheep, graze:
health and happiness.

Sheep, pushing themselves:
suffering.

Shepherd, seeing:
caution in ventures.

Shepherd, seeing with a herd:
gaining wealth.

Shelter from the rain:
hidden annoyance.

Shelter, seeking from enemies:
fraud.

Ship, building:
grandiose, giant projects.

Ship, burning:
huge losses.

Ship, fighting the waves:
lots of conflict with your enemies.

Ship, in harbour:
no change of your task.

Ship, machinery, seeing:
unexpected messages from your creditors.

Ship, sailing under a bridge:
approaching danger, and luckily overcoming it.

Ship, seeing or being on it:
unexpected good news.

Ship, sinking:
frightened by sad news.

Ship, stranded:
big embarrassment.

Ship, with many passengers:
emigration.

Ship, without sail or mast:
rescue from trouble, misery.

Shirt, taking off:
frustrated hope.

Shirt, torn, seeing:
means good success.

Shirt, seeing:
forthcoming prosperity.

Shirt, washing or ironing, seeing:
striving for affection.

Shock (terror):
joyful news.

Shoe, buying:
overly hasty.

Shoe, cutting apart:
getting bad, sore feet.

Shoe, fitting:
for your business, suitable undertakings.

Shoe, new, trying on:
good omen.

Shoe, sole, losing:
trouble, inconvenience ahead.

Shoe, too tight, putting on:
hard depression.

Shoemaker, seeing:
troublesome life.

Shooting:
through endurance, reaching your goal.

Shopping:
advantage, gain.

Shore, going for a walk:
getting yourself into danger.

Shot, hearing:
complications.

Shotgun and shooting:
anger, false hopes of profit.

Shoulder, broken:
unpleasantness.

Shoulder, deformed:
loving other women.

Shoulder, shrug:
doubt about your plans.

Shoulders, extremely high:
strength and patience.

Shoulders, swollen:
annoyance from your loved ones.

Shovel, seeing or using:
getting unrewarding work.

Shroud, seeing:
long-lasting illness.

Shrub (bush), seeing:
falling in love quickly.

Shrub or bushes, cutting down:
seeing unpleasantness diminish.

Shrub or bushes, hurting you:
losses in business.

Shrub or bushes, walking through quite some distance:
obstacles of different kinds.

Siblings, seeing deceased:
long life.

Siblings, seeing dying:
losing enemies.

Sick, and being in pain:
misery and bad luck.

Sickness, suffering from a hidden one:
dishonourable wealth.

Sick people, visiting and comforting:
joy, cheerfulness, happiness.

Sickle, seeing or using:
profit.

Sickle, sharpening:
pleasant messages.

Side of your body, being swollen or injured:
great wealth and happiness.

Sieve, seeing:
an unanswered request.

Sign, seeing:
involvement in disputes.

Sign, plate of an inn:
beware of rivalry.

Signpost:
coming into a tricky situation.

Silk dress, wearing:
entering desired status in society.

Silk dress, tearing:
not knowing a good thing when it's offered to you.

Silk, red colour, seeing:
forthcoming casualty.

Silk, seeing or using:
flourishing business.

Silkworm, finding or seeing:
many truthful friends.

Silk material, woven:
hesitation in your course of business.

Silver, seeing:
pursuit by false friends, decieved by your lover.

Silver, dishes:
coming into fine situations.

Silver, small coins, seeing:
unpleasantness, losses.

Silver, precious metals, seeing or receiving:
joy, money and possessions.

Silver things, wearing:
    servitude.

Silver pieces, your own:
    difficulty.

Silver pieces, selling off:
    improvement in business.

Single, being:
    union.

Singing:
    you will hear uncomfortable things.

Singing, hearing:
    good news will come from far distant friends or relatives.

Singing in the bathtub:
    losing your voice.

Singing in front of a sovereign:
    becoming critical, fault finding.

Singing, nice songs with a clear voice:
    everyone is well and happy.

Singing with a fun crowd:
    getting opinions from many different people.

Siskin, seeing or hearing:
    be steadfast in your plans.

Sisters or brothers, seeing or talking to:
    annoyance, disagreements.

Skating:
    success.

Skating, seeing:
    interruptions in your business.

Skeleton, seeing:
    shock, frightened.

Skeleton, animal, seeing:
    arguments, quarrel about pedantry.

Skeleton (bones), seeing:
    trouble and unpleasantness.

Skeleton key, seeing:
being robbed.

Skin, eczema:
careful, danger to your health.

Skin, dark coloured or black, seeing or your own:
being cheated by friends or relatives and left behind.

Skirt, too tight, wearing:
experiencing hardship.

Skirts, full of spots:
defamation, slander.

Skull (cross-bones), seeing:
finding out about hidden things.

Sky, clear, blue, sunny, seeing:
lots of joy, being lucky in ventures, your partner takes you to the altar.

Sky, cloudy, red or dark, seeing:
vexation, feud, annoyance with your superior.

Sky, flying up to:
modest wishes are being granted.

Sky, lots of clouds:
unfaithfulness.

Sky, seeing the sun:
discovering clarity in a twisted matter.

Slap in the face:
keeping evil company.

Slapping someone:
peace and calm in your family, good progress in your approach to love.

Slate:
effort completes your task.

Slaughterhouse, seeing, or being in:
fatal projects.

Slaves, seeing:
imprisonment.

Sled:
fun, amusement that doesn't satisfy.

Sleep (cap), hat:
your leisure is damaging.

Sleep, being disturbed in it:
annoyance.

Sleeping in a car:
experiencing unease and worried times.

Sleeping in a church:
neglecting your business.

Sleeping in a gazebo:
promising future.

Sleeping with an ugly person:
ill humoured, sickness.

Sleeping with your parents:
happiness, honour, contentment.

Sleepwalker, seeing:
becoming ill.

Sleepwalking:
imminent accident.

Sleeve, taking apart:
divisions.

Sleeves, having wide ones:
acquaintance.

Sleeves, long, seeing:
great honour.

Sleeves, losing:
return to the beginning, starting all over again.

Slippers, worn out:
annoyance.

Slippers, wearing, walking in:
good conscience, inner peace.

Sloughy, stepping in or seeing:
effortless and hard work.

Smallpox, having or seeing:
　　receiving money from unexpected circumstances.

Smell, good fragrance:
　　loyal friendship.

Smell, odour, bad:
　　unfaithfulness, phoniness from others.

Smoke, coming through a chimney:
　　keeping an engagement and being present.

Smoke, seeing:
　　happiness just for show, deception.

Smuggler:
　　entanglement, complications.

Snail, seeing:
　　good news.

Snake, being bitten by:
　　disturbance in a happy relation.

Snake, killing:
　　get rid of a rival.

Snake, seeing:
　　female enemy, being decieved.

Snare (trap), seeing:
　　betrayal.

Snipe, eating:
　　sadness, acquaintance with false and ungrateful friends.

Snipe, flying:
　　experiencing lots of changes.

Snow, seeing, walking through:
　　prospect of multiple luck, flourishing business.

Snow balls, throwing:
　　injuring your body.

Snowflakes, falling:
　　receiving fine promises.

Soap, using or seeing:
　　straightening out messy business, being supported by
　　friends and relatives.

Soap bubbles, blowing:
enjoying brief happiness.

Soap, piece of:
vanity creates damage.

Solar eclipse:
war and hard times.

Soldiers pursuing you:
unrest and bad luck.

Soliciting:
difficulties and misery in the family.

Solicitor, asking you for charity:
cheerfulness.

Solicitor, seeing:
troublesome future.

Solicitor, entering a house:
vexation, annoyance.

Solicitor, sending away:
misery, deficiency, often also prison.

Solicitors, giving something:
success in all ventures, without efforts returning love.

Soot, finding in your meal:
annoyance.

Soup:
hard consistent work, provides plenty to live on.

Sown, seeing or doing it:
wealth, happiness and health.

Spark, flying around:
tendency to extravagance.

Sparrow, seeing lots together:
ruin.

Sparrow hawk, catching:
triumph over your enemies.

Spear, seeing:
hate and hostility.

Spectacle (show), seeing or attending:
happiness in marriage, success in deeds.

Spelling, learning:
for those who work, good; for the lazy, bad.

Spider, seeing:
lawsuit.

Spiders:
annoyance, depression, sadness.

Spider, killing:
losing money.

Spider web:
someone is trying to get a secret out of you.

Spine, broken:
losing money, friends, death of a dear relative.

Spine, a long one:
derision, scoffing.

Sponge, to wash yourself, using or seeing:
treason, greed.

Sponge, burning, taking out of your pocket:
escaping danger of fire.

Spoon, seeing:
being invited as a guest.

Spoon, silver, wearing:
great wealth.

Sprinter:
precipitance gets you in trouble.

Spruce, seeing or standing under:
being fooled or tricked.

Spurge:
confide in a disloyal person.

Spy:
beware of unfaithfulness.

Squirrel, seeing:
for a single woman, good marriage; for a married person, worries about your children.

Squirrel, biting you:
for a single person, bad husband; for a married person, bad children.

Stabbed:
fear and danger.

Stable, being there:
bondage.

Stable, with nice livestock:
prosperity.

Stag (deer), seeing:
gain, profit.

Stain, dress:
sadness.

Stairs, seeing:
joy, advantage.

Stairs, walking down:
treasures obtaining.

Stairs, waking up:
sorrow.

Stake (post):
defiance.

Stalk (following):
dangerous intention.

Starlings:
pleasant, joyful news.

Stars, seeing in the sky:
luck in love, joyful news from friends or relatives.

Stairs, in huge numbers, seeing:
very happy omen.

Stars or shooting stars falling:
unexpected happiness awaits you.

Statue, seeing:
embarrassment.

Statue, tipped over, seeing:
departure.

Steam engine, seeing:
> great wealth.

Steam ship, traveling on:
> bringing an affair or matter, fast to an end.

Stealing, from you:
> loss of friends.

Stick:
> coming under a strict leader.

Stirrup, seeing:
> soon going on an early trip.

Stock (inventory), taking:
> receiving an inheritance.

Stockings, out of silk, putting on:
> poverty.

Stockings, out of cotton or linen:
> changeable luck.

Stockings, pulling down:
> returning happiness.

Stockings, with holes:
> happiness for show, pretending.

Stomach, seeing:
> casualties.

Stone, precious, seeing:
> falling into temptation.

Stone, precious, own:
> great honour.

Stone, precious, receiving:
> increasing wealth.

Stone, precious, wearing:
> arrogance.

Stone carver:
> reward for a deserved deed.

Stone, cutting in a quarry:
> obtaining property, real-estate.

Stones, seeing, walking over:
    struggle and suffering.

Store, with lots of merchandise:
    significant business.

Stork, seeing:
    happy marriage, many children who have turned out well.

Storm, being in it:
    bad luck in love, unfaithfulness.

Storm and rain, experiencing:
    your wishes come true.

Storm, and trees falling:
    avoiding huge disaster.

Stove, glowing:
    becoming lavish, prodigal.

Stove, seeing:
    disaster and separation.

Stove pipe, seeing:
    small losses.

Strangers, talking to or seeing:
    honour and development in your business.

Straw bundle:
    prosperity.

Straw mat:
    moderation keeps you healthy.

Straw, on fire:
    luck and flourishing business.

Straw roof, seeing:
    through misfortune becoming poor.

Straw scattered:
    misery and annoyance.

Strawberries, eating or seeing:
    joy about your children, late, but good marriage, success in
    business, long-lasting health.

Strawberries, seeing lots:
    growing friendship.

Strawberries, huge, seeing:
> pride.

Strawberries, giving away:
> means that you will be well remembered.

Strawberries, picking nice, big ones:
> great joy.

Street ballad, singing:
> acquaintances brings you into difficulty.

Street, long with nice houses:
> being surprised by something beautiful, friendly reception.

Street, with many people:
> you will get lots of business.

Stretcher:
> means death.

Studying:
> long-lasting joy.

Stutter, stammer:
> making a strong resolution.

Suburb, seeing:
> getting a little profit.

Suitcase, seeing:
> forthcoming trip.

Sully and cleaning yourself:
> escaping from danger.

Sully, by someone else:
> defamation, slander.

Sully, yourself:
> unfaithfulness.

Sulphur, seeing:
> false rumours abolishing, clearing your name.

Sulphur, striking (as in a match):
> imminent, serious illness.

Sulphur, handling:
> poor income ahead.

Sun, shining bright:
>luck in enterprises, gaining wealth, a position in public office.

Sun, shining in your bed:
>serious illness.

Sun, becoming dark:
>a bad omen, obstacles in business.

Sun, falling from the sky:
>means death of a dignitary.

Sun, reflecting in water:
>empty promises.

Sunflower:
>honour and prestige.

Sun (or rain) umbrella, seeing or using:
>finding support, recommended by sponsors.

Sunrise, glowing red:
>imminent accident.

Sunset, beautiful seeing:
>a peaceful, cheerful life.

Sunset, glow:
>regain your health.

Swallow, seeing:
>a merry message, luck in love.

Swallows, hearing twitter:
>settlement in a started dispute.

Swallows nesting in or outside of your house:
>steadfast and growing harmony and happiness in your family.

Swallows, flying in swarms:
>having a large family.

Swallows, nest:
>happy family and rewarding business.

Swamp, stepping into:
>misfortune, annoyance in business.

Swans, seeing:
happiness in your marriage, many children, a long and
happy life. For a lover, truthful and faithful returning love.

Swearing, or someone else is swearing:
unpleasant news, sadness.

Sweeping your rooms:
patience in ventures, joyful success.

Sweeping dirt, stepping into:
difficulty, trouble in you household.

Sweets, candy, chocolates, eating:
advantage, benefit.

Swellings, tumour, seeing or having:
wealth and riches.

Swimming and sinking:
disaster and prosecution.

Swimming in clear water:
luck and continuous business.

Swimming in cloudy water:
bad omen.

Swimming and having your life in danger:
rescue from danger and trouble.

Swimming and reaching shore:
an almost impossible dream, seeing it come true.

Swimming and rescuing someone:
escaping a great danger.

Sword, own or having:
experiencing honour.

Sword, nice, polished, receiving:
power, controlling others.

Sword, losing:
losing your established respect.

Sword, breaking apart:
very bad omen.

Sword, with soft handle, getting as a gift:
forthcoming great honour.

ℑ

Table, seeing decorated:
> great joy.

Table, setting:
> prosperity and wealth.

Tail, seeing:
> being insulted.

Tailor, at his job:
> fraud and treason.

Tallow (candle), making or seeing:
> achieving rest and peace of mind.

Tankard, seeing:
> drinking is harmful.

Tar:
> be careful, tricky company people around you.

Task, officially having or getting:
> enduring losses.

Tea, drinking or having:
> unclear business.

Tea kettle:
> unpleasant messages will surprise you.

Teacher, seeing or talking:
> being cheated.

Teeth, losing them:
> through death losing friends or otherwise unexpected misfortune.

Teeth, cleaning:
> struggle for others.

Telegraph pole, seeing:
> going on a distant trip.

Tenant, seeing:
> good social standing, being well-off.

Tent, seeing:
> your job is not secure.

Testament:
(see Last Will)

Testimony:
being in favour by a distinguished, noble person.

Theatre:
invitation to parties.

Thermometer:
unstable friendship.

Thieves, breaking in:
good luck and security in business deals.

Thigh, your own broken:
dying far from your family, marrying in a foreign country.

Thigh, having nice ones:
luck on trips or undertakings.

Thighs, seeing extremely strong ones:
family and honour.

Thighs, seeing nice white ones:
health and happiness.

Thimble, wearing:
hard work and effort are in vain.

Thin (skinny), yourself being:
strong health.

Thirst, cannot be quenched:
endless efforts in some matters, sadness and unrest.

Thirst, to quench in excess:
happiness, honour and great wealth.

Thistles, seeing:
treason, betrayal.

Thorns, being pricked by:
withdrawing from an acquaintance.

Thread, unwinding:
discovery of a secret.

Thread, entangle:
secrets are well protected.

Thread, seeing:
> infatuate, charming.

Thresh, seeing:
> efforts are in vain.

Throat, seeing:
> your hopes are being fulfilled.

Throne:
> coming to honour and authority.

Thunder and lightening, hearing or seeing:
> means being chased into fear.

Thunder and lightening, no damage caused:
> happy reunion from a boy- or girlfriend.

Thunder and lightening, catching fire:
> indicates losses, before long.

Thunder, without lightening:
> a merry message.

Thunder storm:
> bad news.

Tie, seeing:
> vanity creates heartbreak.

Tied-up:
> invitation to a rendezvous.

Tin, seeing:
> illness.

Tinder:
> danger ahead.

Tinker, seeing:
> arguments with your neighbours.

Tidbit, enjoying:
> lack of moderation makes you sick.

Toad, seeing:
> losing friends, fraud, pursuit by enemies.

Toad, killing:
> triumph over enemies.

Tobacco box:
improving health.

Tobacco, handing out:
annoyance.

Tobacco, taking, inhaling:
forthcoming thirst for pleasure, sex.

Tobacco, pipe, smoking:
success.

Tobacco, pipe, seeing:
arguments.

Tobacco, pipe, breaking apart:
reconciliation with an enemy.

Toilet, lavatory:
annoyance, boredom.

Tongue, seeing:
enduring slander and malignity.

Toys, seeing:
stay away from childishness.

Tools, seeing:
lots of rewarded work ahead.

Toothache:
after sorrow, follows joy.

Toothpick, using or seeing:
very bad omen.

Toothbrush:
a screening in your social circle is necessary.

Torch, carrying:
means you are being loved.

Torch, glowing:
shedding light on mysterious, vague subject matter.

Torch, seeing falling from the sky:
headache.

Torch, put out:
destroying a comfortable relation.

Torture, suffering from:
lots of distress.

Towel, seeing:
relief from unpleasant people.

Tower, collapsing:
imminent misfortune.

Tower bells, hearing:
you will soon hear pleasant news.

Towers, seeing them in gold:
envy and hate.

Tower, decorated with stone ornaments:
huge advantage.

Trade, trading:
cheating in a business matter.

Trading, bargaining:
business prosperity.

Train, riding on:
fast developing matters.

Trap door:
unexpected good fortune.

Trap, seeing:
wickedness will be clarified.

Travel bag:
a long trip soon takes place.

Treasure of tremendous value, finding:
death or shame.

Treasure, to own or discover:
betrayal by your best friend.

Tree, falling down from:
loss of job, favoritism and prestige.

Tree, garden, seeing:
richness, great wealth.

Tree, harvesting fruits from an old one:
inheritance.

Tree, roots, seeing:
becoming ill.

Tree, seeing green and in full bloom:
joy, unexpected enjoyment, happy marriage.

Tree, seeing one which is dry:
death, dying.

Tree, seeing yourself high up in:
power and honour, good news.

Tree, sitting under:
good news.

Tree, split by lightening:
separation of two lovers.

Trees, fallen, destroyed by lightening or burned in half:
annoyance, fear, anxiety, pain, despair.

Trees, logging:
misfortune.

Trees, on fire:
family quarrels.

Trees, picking leaves or fruit:
casualties, losses, illness.

Trees, without leaves, seeing:
finishing business transactions.

Trees, with lots of fruit, seeing:
profit, wealth.

Trip, making:
avoiding vexation.

Trousers:
error, mistake.

Trout (fish), seeing in water:
cheerfulness and love will enhance your life to come.

Trumpets, hearing:
meeting again, reunion or astonishment.

Trumpet, playing:
hoping for employment.

Turkey (bird), seeing:
    being freed from a miserable situation.

Turks, seeing:
    laziness will hurt you.

Tulips, seeing many beautiful ones:
    changing your living standard.

Tulips, having in your room:
    coming into better conditions.

Turnpike:
    all kinds of obstacles coming your way.

Turtle dove:
    unshakable love and friendship.

Turtle, eating:
    finally reaching your goal after putting forth effort for a
    long time.

Turtle, seeing:
    cherish a secret joy.

U

Udder, of a cow:
    blessings, gift.

Ulna, seeing:
    receiving gifts.

Umbrella:
    caution when alone, prevention of harm.

Undressing:
    bad news.

Uniform, polished, wearing or seeing:
    coming to great honour, promotion.

Uplifting, seeing yourself:
    great honour.

Urinating:
    disagreement.

Urinating and wetting the bed:
   clarifying confusing matters.

Urine, drinking:
   getting into expenses.

Urn, seeing:
   danger ahead.

V

Vail, wearing:
   being respected and loved.

Vampire:
   you are slipping into the influence of a swindler.

Vase, with beautiful flowers:
   gaining wealth.

Vases, breaking:
   losing your boyfriend or girlfriend.

Vat (tub), seeing filled with wine:
   good income.

Vat (tub), seeing full but cannot be used:
   means death in the family.

Vegetables, raw, seeing or eating:
   troubled business, annoyance, sickness.

Vehicle, riding in it:
   prosperity.

Vehicle, carriage, nice one:
   getting to know noble people.

Vehicle, stepping out of it:
   loss of job or dignity.

Vehicle, seeing:
   effort leads to making a good living.

Vehicle, seeing turned over:
   imminent casualties.

Vehicle wheel:
embarrassment.

Vein, huge one, seeing:
scare about your heart.

Velvet:
haughtiness, arrogance brings you down.

Vetch:
your modesty wins you new friends.

Villages, places, seeing:
attending a merry, joyful gathering.

Villages, seeing well-off and kept:
happiness.

Villages, poor, visiting:
losing respect, experiencing disdain, contempt.

Villager, seeing or talking to:
merry days ahead.

Vinegar, drinking:
annoyance, dispute in the household, disagreements.

Vinegar, making:
your mind is brewing about evil things.

Vinegar, red, seeing:
abuse.

Vinegar, seeing:
being offended.

Vinegar, spilling:
being accepted with skepticism, disliked.

Vineyard, seeing or walking through:
prosperity, happy family, accommodating friends.

Vintage, gathering:
happiness, honour and riches.

Violets, seeing in summertime:
wealth and honour.

Violets, not yet in bloom:
lawsuit, losing friends and estate.

Violets, seeing in full bloom:
rewarding efforts.

Violin, seeing:
pleasant company.

Violin, holding or playing:
calmness, patience, unpleasant situation.

Viper, seeing:
lucky in love, great wealth.

Visiting someone:
bearing injustice.

Visitors, expecting:
uncomfortable situation ahead.

Vomit, yourself:
for poor people, good omen; for rich people, disadvantage and damage.

Vulture (falcon), seeing:
malicious illness.

W

Wafer, seeing:
a wished for message, soon to receive.

Waffle:
your thirst for pleasure brings harm.

Walking alone, being lonely:
changeable luck.

Walking and hesitating:
losses and obstacles in business.

Walking, constantly:
careful in your approach.

Walking fast:
taking on your task without hesitation.

Walking with friends:
stability.

Walking with your lover:
unstable relation.

Wall, collapsing:
>   misfortune for you or your family.

Wall, in front of you:
>   annoyance and struggle.

Wall, jumping down from:
>   joy and fun.

Wall, standing on:
>   means huge success.

Wall, surrounded by water:
>   coming into disgrace.

Wallpaper, seeing:
>   joyful news.

Wanderer (traveller):
>   forthcoming trip.

War cry:
>   happiness, prayers and wishes are being answered.

War armament:
>   very bad omen.

War (going to):
>   conflict with your superior.

Warehouse, being in it:
>   means betrayal in the open, pursuit.

Wart:
>   ill-wishing people are getting you in trouble.

Wash basin:
>   cleanliness is the foundation of health.

Washing, watching:
>   libel, slander.

Wasps:
>   unpleasant complications.

Watch, pocket watch:
>   good omen.

Water, seeing bright and clear:
>   prosperity and happiness.

Water, seeing calm and cloudy:
> life is in danger, illness.

Water, warm, drinking:
> rejection by friends, sickness.

Water, walking through:
> rescue from danger.

Water, having over you:
> advantage.

Water, walking on it:
> flourishing success.

Water, in a broken glass, cloth or something that cannot contain it:
> bad luck, losses, dishonour.

Water, pure and clear, being offered in a glass:
> soon to be married, happy childbirth.

Water pail:
> unpleasantness, will be removed.

Water, mill, seeing or being on it:
> happiness, wealth, honour

Water snakes:
> recovering of the ill and sick.

Water, roaring and sweeping:
> bad luck on trips.

Water, being pushed into:
> grief and worries.

Water nymph, seeing:
> treason, prosecution.

Watering can, seeing:
> do not go for extravagances.

Wax:
> be patient and wait, victory is yours.

Ways, seeing many:
> your life will be pleasant.

Weasel, seeing:
> malice will harm you.

Weaving, mill:
> lots of luck in speculative operations.

Wedding, seeing:
> jealousy, lingering illness.

Wedding, having:
> damage, losses.

Wedding, marrying another woman when your wife is still alive:
> confusion in your plans.

Wedding, attending and seeing dancing:
> means deep sorrow.

Wedding, attending:
> joy and good news.

Wedlock:
> prosperity, happiness.

Weeds, seeing:
> enduring losses.

Weep:
> losing a friend for a long time, sorrow and grief.

Weep, to see someone:
> comfort.

Well, seeing with clear water:
> sincere confession.

Well, strong current:
> fire danger.

Well, bathing in clear water:
> escaping from danger.

Well, seeing with beautiful architecture:
> receiving nice gifts.

Well, falling into:
> in fear of the future.

Well, taking water out:
> good business deals.

Whale, seeing:
> huge disaster.

Wheat:
> hard work brings prosperity.

Wheat field in bloom:
> wealth and honourable love, all wishes coming true in marriage, many well-mannered children.

Wheel or wheelwork, seeing:
> forthcoming illness.

Wheels, seeing in action:
> quickly reaching your hoped for goal.

Wheel of fortune, seeing:
> misfortune or annoyance.

Wheelbarrow, being pulled by dogs:
> despair.

Whet (stone), seeing:
> good results in trading.

Whey, drinking:
> worrying about your health.

Whip, seeing:
> beware of punishment.

Whip, swinging:
> making friends through honesty.

Whistle, trying to but can't:
> obstacles in your plans.

Whistle, hearing:
> being warned about something.

Whiskers, having on yourself:
> idle, transient joy.

White grouse, flying:
> unexpected news.

Whore, seeing or talking to:
> happy days ahead, luck.

Whorehouse, seeing:
> misfortune, pursuit, illness.

Widow:
> getting satisfaction.

Wife, talking to:
 unstable changes in business.

Wig:
 vanity brings you sorrow.

Will-o-the-wisp:
 seduction and dishonesty are harmful.

Wind, feeling:
 good event, joyful news.

Window, at the rear side of a building, on fire:
 losing close relatives.

Window, at the front, on fire:
 death of a relative or acquaintance.

Window, climbing out:
 bad luck in business.

Window, seeing open:
 happiness in your household.

Window, seeing closed:
 means things are coming down hard on you

Window, you falling out:
 means lawsuits.

Window, stepping through:
 indicates being good and friendly accepted.

Windowpane, seeing:
 complicated situation.

Wine, spill:
 losing respect.

Wine, seeing:
 hemorrhage warning.

Wine, drinking a good one:
 showing resistance

Wine, mixed with water, drinking:
 illness or changing luck in business.

Wine soup, eating:
 indisposition.

Wine and getting drunk:
receiving love and respect from a noble superior,
happiness in the future.

Wings, having and flying:
good for everybody.

Wire, plain, seeing:
traps being set.

Wire, made out of copper:
a profitable, lucky, ongoing business.

Witch, seeing:
being involved with a greedy person.

Wives, seeing many:
change, variations.

Wolf, biting you:
slander, libel.

Wolf, killing:
getting rid of a bad, tricky enemy.

Women, fooling around with:
dispute about inheritance.

Women, seeing beautiful ones and being in love:
happiness, health and wealth.

Women, old with white hair:
losses of many kinds.

Women, seeing pregnant:
good news.

Women, unknown, seeing or talking to:
acquaintance.

Women, courting:
being cheated by flatterers.

Women, seeing with brown hair:
illness.

Women, seeing with red hair:
being pursued.

Women, seeing with beautiful, long hair:
honour and wealth, happy union.

Women, seeing with black hair:
> uneasiness and sorrow.

Women, being favoured by them:
> arguments ahead.

Women having more than one:
> being tormented.

Women, wearing cloth:
> sorrow, misfortune.

Women, (broad) being in the company of:
> gossip, inconsistency.

Wood, cutting:
> diligence, thrive, prosper.

Wood, carrying:
> becoming poor.

Wood, logging:
> a death.

Wood, picking up or seeing piled up:
> grief, a lot of affliction.

Woodframing:
> great honour.

Wood, throwing into the fire:
> waste, extravagance.

Wood, floating on water:
> devastation about a longed for happiness.

Wooden shoes, seeing or wearing:
> modest, but happy family life.

Wooden vessel, seeing:
> economical - modesty keeps you away from starvation

Wool, buying or selling:
> luck in business, making good money, respect from
> authorities.

World ending:
> stupidity creates obstacles.

Working:
> a good continuation in ventures.

Worms, seeing:
careful - evil is around you.

Worms, killing:
set free from a drawback.

Wound (sore), seeing or being wounded yourself:
good prospect in projects, harmony in the family, false friends are giving up on you.

Wounded person, seeing:
your lack of consideration means disadvantage to others.

Wreath, carrying:
means, mark of salute.

Wreath, making:
diligent.

Wreath made of myrtle, seeing:
wedding.

Wreath, woven from evergreens:
fulfillment of your hopes.

Wreath, seen at a funeral or by graves:
inheritance, or losing your loved ones.

Wrestle:
quarrel and dispute.

Wrestle with a stranger:
imminent danger.

Wrestle with a beast:
defamation.

Wrinkles in your face, seeing:
reaching an old age.

Writer, in an office or public office:
coming into a confusing situation.

Wrought-iron, making:
dispute, argument.

Wrought-iron, seeing or being hit:
great losses.

Wrought-iron, seeing red hot:
intimate love, high blood pressure, nervousness.

Yard, seeing messy:
    disparage.

Yard, span a net over it:
    great wealth.

Yard or farm, owning:
    rich inheritance.

Yarn, entangled:
    lovers chasing each other.

Yarn, to unwind:
    prone to lavishness, to discover a secret.

Yarn, to wind up:
    becoming greedy.

Yasmine (gazebo):
    soon to be an engagement.

Yeast, eating:
    prolonging physical suffering.

Young, becoming:
    vanity causes heartbreak.

Youth, seeing a young man:
    only your own strength leads to prosperity.

Zebra, seeing:
    don't befriend fools.

Zero (number), seeing:
    riches, wealth, honour, good fortune in ventures.

Zither, playing:
    pleasant appearance in society.

Meaning of Dreams According to the Zodiac

There are many dreams that are independent of time and place and have their own meaning. And yet, the same dream could have different meanings, depending on which Zodiac sign the Earth was in when the dream occurred.

To determine more information about a dream in relation to the Zodiac, you must first remember the theme, or main point of the dream. Then, you have to determine (using an astrological calendar) which sign the Earth was in at the time that you had the dream. Once you've done this, you can use the following chart to discover the meaning behind the dream.

For example:

If you dream about a visit from a good friend when the Earth is in Leo, look at the chart under number 9 and then move over to Leo. Your dream means "Honour."

If you dream about music and instruments when the Earth is in Capricorn, look at the chart under number 14, and then move over to Capricorn. Your dream means "Comfort."

Kind of Dream Dreaming of:	1 Aries	2 Taurus	3 Gemini	4 Cancer	5 Leo
1. Money and all kinds of Coins	Illness	Punish-ment	Loss of a Friend	Visitor	Money
2. Fish and aquatic animals	Anxiety	Comfort	Honour	Mental-suffer-ing	Anxiety or Harm
3. Kisses, caresses	Unpleas-antness	Trip	Visitor	A Friend	Advantage, and profit
4. Large Gathering	News	Have dispute	Emotion	Joy	Gift
5. Illness, physical discomfort	Joyful surprise	Joy	Cheat	Losses	Noble Friends
6. Meals, and edible Foods	Joy	Visitors	Joy	Annoy-ance	Long lasting Life
7. Misfortunes of all kinds	Request in vain	Lies	Respectful to others	Weakness	Afflic-tion Grief
8. Churches, Houses, Towers, Buildings in general	Joy	Anguish of mind	Serious Illness	Money	Soon to get Visitors
9. Arrival or visiting of good Friends	Gift	Secret enjoyment	Pleasant-ness	Gain, Profit	Honour
10. Fire, Thunder, and shooting	Sadness	Guests	Profit	Drunk-eness	Losses
11. Fire, (any type of)	Sadness	Misery & Grief	Weakness	Afflic-tion	Rule, mastery, control
12. Body weakness, painfull joints	Good Things	Sadness	Sorrow	Hopes in Vain	New Friendship alliance

6 Virgo	7 Libra	8 Scorpio	9 Sagittarius	10 Capricorn	11 Aquarius	12 Pisces
Cheerful-fulness	Death of a Relative	Theft	Joy	Joy	Losses	Effort
Death of a Friend	Health	Pleasant surprise	Sorrow	Hostility	Illness	Illness
Kindness, good	Invitation	News	Fraud	Loneli-ness	Strange joy	Changing opinion
Happiness	Misfor-tune	Joy	Enjoy-ment	Loss of a friend	Love-affair	Lots of joy
Merryness	Comfort	Dispute	Unhappy love	A Friend	Effort	Worries
Illness	Appre-hension	Fear anxiety	Comfort	Profit	Have arguments	Joy
Trouble deficiency	Illness of a friend	Losses	Winning over a new friend	Pain	Pleasant-ness	Anxious
Lots of Luck	Advantage	Joy	A Friend	Afflic-tion grief	Restless-ness.	Good news
Fear, fright	Sadness, grief	Wealth	Honour	Important event	Sadness	Anger
Sadness	Joy	Weakness	Illness	Visitor	Pain	Great fear
Gain, profit	Surprise	Death	Death	Dispute	Marriage	Joy
Joy	Worry, grief	Illness	Cheerful-ness	Need, distress	Money	Expenses

Kind of Dream Dreaming of:	1 Aries	2 Taurus	3 Gemini	4 Cancer	5 Leo
13. Work-equipment, Tools or instruments	Dispute, money	Profit	Good Things	Gain through a death case	Very pleasant Visitors
14. Singing, music, playing of instruments	Very bad news	Travel	Unexpected Joy	Sadness	Deception
15. Tears, and deep sorrow	Arguments about religion	Vain worries, fear	Joy	Illness	Profit
16. Arguments, dispute, fights, war	Weakness	Victory over your enemy	Very comfort- able	Honour	Envy
17. Dead bodies, funeral	Marriage	Winning in the Lottery	Misfortune	Dispute	Profit
18. Urinating	Losses	Sadness	Idle hopes	Annoyance	Delight
19. Exile, expulsion, abuse	Fraud	Joy	Good things	Guests	Gift
20. Giants, ghosts, monsters	Anxiety	Dispute	Moral aberration	Well being	Illness
21. Horses, huge animals, riders, drivers	Weakness	Honour	Loosing a friend	Surprise	Long life
22. Murder, killing, bloodshed	Grief, deep sorrow	Loss of a friend	Intimacy, familiarity	Richness, wealth	Illness
23. Joy, Cheerfulness, entertainment	Sorrow, affliction	Foolish- ness	Money	Cheerful- ness	Envy
24. New, fine cloth, linen sheets	Intoxi- cation	Joy	Annoyance	Guests or dinner party	Hostility

6 Virgo	7 Libra	8 Scorpio	9 Sagittarius	10 Capricorn	11 Aquarius	12 Pisces
A Girl-friend	Theft	Honour	Unpleasant news	Worries	Comfort	News
Strange events	Fooled hopes	Grief through a	Aquaint-ance	Comfort	Pleasant things	Argument
Joy	Pleasing surprise	Amuse-ment, fun	Fright	Death of a relative	Death of a superior	Enemies
Pleasing things	Welcome message	Good money making	Pleasing news	Dispute	Being merry	Tears
Disagree-ment	Grief, worries	Joy	Shock, terror	Surprise	Enormous luck	Lottery-win
Illness	Joy	Fright	War	Unexpected friends	Love	Happiness
Grief	Bad things	Death of a relative	Move, moving	Guests	Hostility	Joy
Money	Joyful, happy	Death of a friend	Enormous luck	Joy	Joy	Visitor
Argument	Degrading	Sadness	Fraud	Libel, slander	Dinner with guests	Deception
Pain	Concern, trouble	Harm	Soon to be dead	Losses	Fraud	Advantage
Pleasant-ness	Unpleasant-ness	Affliction, distress	Joy	Delight-fulness	Profit	Joy
Dispute	Joy	Honour	Losses	News	Injury, harm	Hostility

Chart of Lucky and
Unlucky Days

Lucky Days

•January	1	3	10	27	31
•February	7	8	18		
•March	5	9	12	14	16
•April	5	17			
•May	1	2	4	9	14
•June	3	5	7	12	25
•July	2	6	10	23	30
•August	4	7	10	14	20
•September	6	10	13	17	30
•October	15	16	25	31	
•November	1	15	25	30	
•December	10	20	29		

Unlucky Days

•January	13	23		
•February	2	10	17	22
•March	13	19	23	28
•April	18	20	29	30
•May	10	17	20	
•June	4	20		
•July	(no dates given)			
•August	5	13	27	31
•September	13	16	18	26
•October	3	9	27	
•November	6	23		
•December	15	26	31	

Birthmonth — Characteristics

January

A male born in January has many talents but little pride. With much effort he will become a real go-getter. He enjoys being around positive people and has much luck and happiness in marriage. He has the potential to strike it rich.

A female born in January can never have enough lovers, despite her cold-hearted feelings. She will marry a well-off man, but will cause trouble for her husband.

February

A male born in February has a strong spiritual drive, as well the ability to handle both physical and spiritual pressure. He loves gambling, riding horses and driving cars. He is careless and foolish, but in the end, he will find happiness.

A female born in February is not very well-read. She pretends to love books, but secretly wishes nothing more than to be mar-

March

A male born in March has an unstable nature, and therefore has difficulty making decisions. Despite his insecurity, he does not stay single. His earnings and acheivements will provide a comfortable lifestyle for him in his old age.

A female born in March loves men very much, but is clever enough to hide her weakness. She is known to visit fortune tellers, and is shocked by things she doesn't want to hear.

April

A male born in April is honourable, witty and pleasure-seeking. His trickster-like character suits him well. He enjoys success in education and employment, but shows little interest in marriage.

A female born in April has a surly, sullen nature. She desires marriage at a young age and has many expectations about her relationship. After her wedding, she will often sing this song:

Those who expect from the golden ring only golden days,
Oh they don't know the course of life,
and not the hearts of men.

May

A male born in May is diligent and skillful, but has a very stubborn character. In his married life he will have a lot of obstacles to overcome.

A female born in May is witty and jolly, but also very conscientious. She wins over many friends, but finds it difficult to acquire wealth.

June

A male born in June shows little interest in education or work. However, he manages to get by with what he inherits from his mother.

A female born in June is very lady-like and able to mask her feelings. She combines female affection with man-like steadfastness. She is good-hearted, but fights back if someone tries to do wrong. She loves money, but manages to live in a modest fashion.

July

A male born in July has many talents but will develop only a few. He has a tendency to boast about his heroism, although much of this is fabricated. He is always speculating and would love nothing more than to find a rich bride.

A female born in July is hungry for knowledge and she studies a lot. Although she does not like to cook, she will be a good housewife. Her husband will have nothing to complain about except her superior intellect.

August

A male born in August has a very jealous nature, but he manages to hide it most of the time. He doesn't have much luck with women. He will live a long life.

A female born in August has a compassionate nature and, therefore, is vulnerable to objectionable happenings. She does not want to remain single.

September

A male born in September has a large ego and is quick to quarrel with others. He does not listen to warnings and has many enemies. However, in marriage he is a loving, caring husband.

A female born in September is always worrying, even when there is nothing to worry about. She is a pet-lover throughout her life, makes her husband very happy and is a good money-manager.

October

A male born in October is cheerful and merry. He is attracted to females from an early age and is drawn to them his whole life. In marriage he can be extremely happy.

A female born in October tends, even at an early age, to play the 'wise guy'. She is more drawn to a high-ranked man than any other one. She is not opposed to marrying a widower without children.

November

A male born in November is very carefree. He likes to play the role of master, and does not hesitate to fabricate stories. In marriage, he has a chance to eliminate some of his mistakes.

A female born in November is naughty and witty, pays a lot of attention to her appearance and never says "no" when being asked for a dance. She prefers the company of men to women, and will marry at a young age.

December

A male born in December is successful in ventures that do not involve a lot of thought. He likes to reach for higher goals, but will always be satisfied with the woman he has chosen.

A female born in December has a tendency to flirt. Even though she receives a great deal of flattery, she shows tremendous steadfastness.

Fingernail – Characteristics

By Colour

Pale and lead-coloured nails. . .
indicate a melancholic person who prefers a quiet
lifestyle that includes studying and spiritual activity.

White nails. . .
indicate a person of thin, dainty stature who enjoys
being in love, but who has stomach problems.

White nails with lead-coloured spots. . .
indicate a person who leans toward a melancholic nature
but is easily irritated.

By Shape

Wide nails. . .
indicate a soft, emotional, warm-hearted person who is
also very shy.

Wide nails surrounded by damaged skin. . .
indicate a person who indulges in risk-free delights and
amusements.

Wide nails with white spots. . .
indicate a very careless person who will let luck run right
through his/her hands.

Fleshy, thick nails. . .
indicate a calm, composed person who loves to sleep, eat
and drink, and who finds enjoyment in the activities of
others.

Long nails. . .

> indicate a well-mannered, good natured person who, according to others, "achieved a good soul of inner peace," but will never become rich.

Round nails. . .

> indicate someone with an angry but good-hearted character who is fond of science. He or she is somewhat willful and conceited about ability and the beauty of their body.

Small nails. . .

> characterize a very nosy person who has the misfortune of having a loose tongue.

Rough nails. . .

> indicate a person with a jolly nature. This person loves to be alive and wishes it will never end.

~··· ···⌣

Epilogue

Over 400 years ago, when Nostradamus first began sharing his knowledge of astrology, astronomy and medicine, and his gift as a seer, he became one of the most respected figures of his time. Not only because he could foretell the future, but also because he accepted the laws of creation as a fact of life. His recognition of the forces of nature, and his ability to understand their connection with our lives, gave him the wisdom that made him so outstanding and unique. He was held in extremely high regard by the people of his time, most of whom could only dream of being blessed with such gifts; rarely did one with such a high standard of knowledge and understanding walk among them.

But that was 400 years ago...

Now, this awareness and knowledge of creation is available to all who strive for it, in the book

IN THE LIGHT OF TRUTH —
The Grail Message,

by ABD-RU-SHIN

"Among all books of spiritual content this work occupies a unique place. It brings the recognition of the all-embracing Laws of Creation, and guides the reader to a profound knowledge of the meaning of existence."

Dr. R. Steinpach

The Author writes:
". . .I wish to fill the gaps which have so far always remained unanswered in the souls of men, and which never leave any serious thinker in peace, if he honestly seeks the Truth."

ABD-RU-SHIN

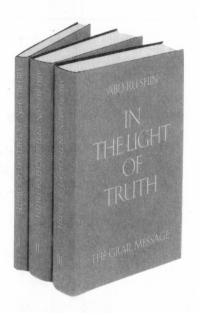

Original edition: German
Also available in: English, French, Italian, Dutch, Portuguese, Spanish, Czech, Russian, Chinese.

On sale in bookstores and from Grail Publications:
(in Canada): Grail Publications, P.O. Box 412, Chénéville, PQ, JOV 1E0, Tel/fax: (819) 428-2898 or 1-800-672-2898
(in US): Grail Foundation Press, P.O.Box 45, Gambier OH, 43022, Tel: 1-800-427-9217; Fax: 1-614-427-4954